THE
GROOM-TO-BE'S
HANDBOOK

THE
GROOM-TO-BE'S
HANDBOOK

THE ULTIMATE GUIDE

TO A FABULOUS RING,

A MEMORABLE PROPOSAL,

AND A PERFECT WEDDING

TODAY'S GROOM **MAGAZINE**

SKYHORSE PUBLISHING

www.skyhorsepublishing.com

All interior art courtesy of www.istockphoto.com

Library of Congress Cataloging-in-Publication Data

The groom-to-be's handbook : the ultimate guide to a fabulous ring,
a memorable proposal, and a perfect wedding / Today's Groom Magazine.
p. cm.
ISBN-13: 978-1-60239-101-7 (alk. paper)
ISBN-10: 1-60239-101-7 (alk. paper)
1. Weddings–Planning. 2. Bridegrooms. 3. Etiquette for men. I. Today's Groom
Magazine.

HQ745.G76 2007
395.2'2–dc22
2007020060
10 9 8 7 6 5 4 3 2 1

Printed in China

CONTENTS

ACKNOWLEDGMENTS

In putting this book together we would like to recognize the major contributors and writers. Jake Beirbaum, Janis Turk, and Peter van der Hagen have compiled their experiences with that of many experts in order to create this great guide for men considering and entering into marriage. These three writers spent countless hours interviewing experts, married couples, and newly engaged couples to give men the help they need, from buying the engagement ring to walking down the aisle. Thank you to Elizabeth Reisinger who worked with us as a contributing editor to this book.

INTRODUCTION

This book is dedicated to you, the man. It is all about you and the decisions you will make along your path to marriage. We will cover everything you need to know, including how to be sure she is "the one" and how to choose the perfect moment to pop the question. You'll find lots of real life proposal stories to inspire you in creating your own unforgettable engagement. We'll walk you through the ring buying experience, from what styles and cuts are out there to how much you really have to spend. What you will *not* find here are shiny pictures of pink bouquets, suggestions for picking out bridesmaid dresses, or tips for finding a gown that flatters your figure. Rest assured—this is a book by guys, for guys.

Our goal is to make life a little easier for you (at least as far as your engagement goes—sorry, there's not much we can do about your favorite sports team's losing streak). After reading this book you should feel confident in taking your relationship to the next level. You will have the knowledge necessary to make an informed decision on purchasing an engagement ring. You will know what you need to do and who you need to talk with prior to your engagement. You will be able to plan a classic or elaborate proposal that will wow the woman of your dreams. Finally, you will know what to expect once the ring is on her finger and the wedding planning begins.

You're welcome for saving you from ever having to look through a flowery bridal magazine for advice or inspiration. We hope you enjoy this book as much as we enjoyed creating it.

PART ONE

SO YOU WANT TO GET MARRIED

—

· I ·

NAVIGATING ENGAGEMENT

ENGAGEMENT 101

- **Think it through.** Proposing to your girlfriend is a major decision. Be sure marriage is what you really want before you commit to it.
- **Know her thoughts, too.** Propose to her when you feel that both of you are ready to take the next step, and you can't go wrong. Use what you know and love about her to create a great proposal.
- **Know why you want her.** Everyone gets married for different reasons. Think about exactly why you want to be married to your girlfriend.
- **Prepare for change.** After you become engaged, your relationship will change. As a fiancé, you will have different obligations.
- **Compromise.** Take inventory of what compromises might be needed to ensure a successful relationship and marriage. It may be easier to have an open discussion about these things before you are married.

HOW TO KNOW IF SHE'S READY

Despite what television sitcoms and the film industry suggest, your girlfriend may not send blatantly obvious clues that reveal when she is ready to marry you. Chances are, she's not going to wave her left hand in your face and demand a ring (if she did, you'd probably run). However, this doesn't mean you should be completely in the dark about her feelings. She may make references to common friends getting married, or you may discover a new bridal magazine where your *Sports Illustrated* used to lay. If she bought you this book, you can be darn sure marriage is on her mind. Subtler clues will come as you evaluate the larger picture of your relationship.

HOW TO TELL IF YOU'RE READY

It is often said that absence makes the heart grow fonder. A far more telling scenario emerges when you have nowhere else to go for an extended period of time, and your girlfriend is never more than a few rooms away. In these situations, do you feel uncomfortable, or are you content being together? We all have that friend who is great for the first hour, but more than that starts making us think like Jack Nicholson in *The Shining*. That shouldn't be the case with your girlfriend. If it is, you will need to learn how to communicate with her about whatever it is that drives you crazy when you're together for too long.

The beginning of any new relationship is an adjustment period. You start off with your best foot forward. You wear dressy clothing, take her on dates to classy restaurants, hold doors open for her, and rein in some other less desirable behaviors. As the relationship progresses, you naturally become more comfortable around her and begin to allow your quirks and eccentricities to emerge. Some men become very laissez-faire. Formal wear is swapped for sweatpants and ripped boxers. They still open doors for her, but the doors belong to McDonald's and Blockbuster. While it's always important to treat the woman you love like a lady, becoming more comfortable with each other is a positive progression. If your girlfriend can love you when you are at your worst, then she really does love you. Feeling secure enough to be yourself around her will be a determining factor in your future.

Your wife should be one of your best friends, if not your best friend. She may not always care about everything you have to say, but she will want to listen because she cares about you. She loves you because of everything that defines you, from your life's aspirations to how you clip your toenails. If you feel the same way about her, you may be ready to promise your life to her.

WHY *N OT* TO GET MARRIED

Pressure. If you feel like you are getting backed into a corner with ultimatums about either getting married or breaking up, then you need to seriously consider your options. Marriage is intended to be a lifelong commitment to each other. If you are not fully invested or just not ready, then despite any good intentions you have, you may be setting yourself up to fail. Buying a home, moving to another state, or joining the military are all major life choices. You wouldn't make a decision about these issues unless you were really sure of what you wanted. So why would you enter into an engagement with any less certainty? You could live in your house for ten years, relocate for a few years, or serve your country for six years, but marriage is intended to last for as long as you both shall live.

To make your relationship stronger. Couples sometimes use marriage as a Band-Aid for their relationship woes. For example, if you know you're not spending enough time together now, you may think that being married will fix that problem. The reality is, if you don't value quality time with each other enough to fit it in your schedule before marriage, you won't after the wedding, either.

QUESTIONS TO ASK

You have to know yourself before you can know if someone is the right life mate for you. This calls for a personal assessment of your values. Do

Who knows where you will be in ten or twenty years? Allow yourself the freedom to change, but don't be pressured into giving up the things that matter most to you in life.

you want children? If so, how many? Would you like them sooner or later in life? Do you expect someone to stay home to care for them? If so, who? If your girlfriend does not want children, are you going to be satisfied without them? How important is religion to you? Would you consider converting to your girlfriend's religion? Could you live with someone whose political views often conflict with your own? Do you feel the need to be established in your career before marriage? Are you worried about your financial situation? These are just a handful of questions that you should ask yourself before you can have a meaningful conversation with your girlfriend about your compatibility.

Be honest with yourself as you think about these questions. Wanting to be married doesn't mean that it is okay to compromise your deepest goals and values. There will be some sacrifices that each of you will have to make, but being forced to give up on your dreams, the core of who you are, will only lead to resentment. Blame can poison a relationship, turning love into hate. There are enough obstacles in life without creating more. Knowing what you can and cannot live with or without will help you to better understand yourself.

Keep in mind that as human beings, we are constantly changing our views and opinions. Just because you wanted to be a fireman in the second grade doesn't mean that you have to choose that life today. Who knows where you will be in ten or twenty years? Allow yourself the freedom to change, but don't be pressured into giving up the things that matter most to you in life.

Many people operate under the assumption that after they find their soul mate, everything else will fall into place and they will live happily ever after. Sorry, but this just isn't the case. As with family and friends, we often fight with each other, because we care enough to voice our differences and work out our problems, rather than thinking it doesn't matter or giving up when we don't immediately get our way. While constant arguing is not good for anyone, understand that problems will occur. Being willing and able to confront issues and learn from them is a key element to any relationship.

There are no guarantees in life, and committing yourself to another person may come down to a decision of faith. It means having faith that during the hard times your wife will be there to support and love you and that you will always do the same for her.

WHAT TO EXPECT ONCE YOU'RE ENGAGED

When contemplating your engagement, you need to realize that after the proposal, your relationship will undoubtedly change. This isn't to say that it will necessarily be better or worse than before—just different. Your new status as her fiancé will increase demands upon your time. It also may be expected that you begin spending more time together, especially more time with your extended families.

During engagement, your relationship progresses through a period of discovering each other's personalities to a time of solidifying your identity as a couple. Your commitment becomes public knowledge. It may change the way you perceive yourself, and it may also change the way your friends and network of acquaintances perceive you. At this time it is appropriate to take a look at your life and create an inventory of what you will be giving up and all that you will be receiving. An engagement is a major stepping stone in a person's life, and it is impor-

> You do not have to agree on everything. However, you should express that while you may disagree with her opinion, you will always care about what she thinks.

tant to acknowledge that there will be sacrifices on both sides of the relationship.

Communication is key. Being able to discuss expectations, misunderstandings, or feelings will help to limit potential problems. Keep in mind that communicating requires both expressing your reasoning and listening to hers. Ignoring either aspect may lead to increased frustration and create secondary issues.

You do not have to agree on everything. However, you should express that while you may disagree with her opinion, you will always care about what she thinks. You may never believe that figure skaters are as athletic as football players, or that *Sex in the City* is a better show than *Seinfeld*. If, after reasonable discussion, each of you still holds to your original opinions, you must simply agree to disagree. At least you won't be required to tune into the next figure skating competition when she knows it will only lead to another argument. If you present your rationale clearly and respectfully, then regardless of the magnitude of the topic, you will build a proper foundation for addressing and resolving future dilemmas.

PRE-PROPOSAL BASICS

Prospective grooms are often torn between the idea of respecting established traditions and creating a proposal that is unique. They wonder if they should follow every custom—from asking for her father's blessing to getting down on one knee while proposing. You may not care at all about how you propose, but maybe your girlfriend has been dreaming of this event her entire life. Perhaps neither of you will have a strong preference, and you may want to make a decision based upon the wishes of family or close friends.

If you are considering proposing, then chances are you have been dating for an extended period of time, or have at least known each other for a while. Think about her personality. Has she responded well to your romantic advances? If so, an elaborate proposal may be just what she is looking for. Is she family-oriented? How often does she talk to her parents? How well do you know her family? Your answers should help you to decide whether or not to ask for her parents' blessing.

Think logically; if she hasn't spoken to her father for many years, then it would be pointless to ask for his blessing. Asking for a blessing is a chance to show your respect for her family, and it can also help to form a closer bond with her parents. You may choose to capitalize on the opportunity by creating an event around the tradition. Prepare and cook a meal for her family, take them to a ball game, or ask her father on a hunting trip (if that's something you are both interested in). Because of all of the possible family configurations, you will have to decide exactly whose blessing to ask for. In some situations, it might be appropriate to ask both parents, while in others you may need to ask only her mother or even her stepfather. A lot of the time, requesting

> When is the right time to propose? This is the easiest question to answer. The right time is quite simply whenever it feels right for the both of you.

a blessing is a mere formality, but treating it as such may undermine your noble intentions. Be honest and respectful, and you won't go wrong.

When is the right time to propose? This is the easiest question to answer. The right time is quite simply whenever it feels right for both of you. If you already know that you both want to be married and have covered all of the important issues, then it would be very difficult to choose an inappropriate time.

You may be able to sense a rhythm to your relationship that points you in the right direction. For others, it may arrive as a kind of epiphany—suddenly you just know that the time is right. If you decide to plan your proposal, then the timing will depend on your choice of action. We will lay down all of our "Rules of Engagement" in the second section of this book and give you some real life stories for guidance and inspiration.

· 2 ·

BEFORE YOU BUY A RING

It is normal to be a little worried about picking out an engagement ring. You probably have questions about how much to spend, payment options, and even what sort of stone to choose. To make it a little less nerve-wracking, we have compiled a few suggestions to ease you into the process.

Keep in mind that your girlfriend will be wearing her ring for the rest of her life. Thinking that you know what type of ring she would like is not the same thing as knowing for sure. If she loves you, she may never tell you that she doesn't like the ring you get her. But the last thing you want is for her to be disappointed. So figure out what she wants (more advice on this later).

Your first question is probably, "How much should I spend?" As men, we often think that women equate the size of the ring with how much we love them. The ring is a symbol of your unending love. No woman wants to feel underappreciated, but she also doesn't want you to bury yourself under a pile of debt. A good rule of thumb is to spend between one and two month's salary on the engagement ring.

However, you may have other financial constraints. If you do not have all of the resources you need when you are ready to make the purchase, it is possible to get a loan to finance a part

Tip

Plan to spend between one and two months' salary on the engagement ring. Consider financing options if you don't have the money up front, but don't get buried in debt.

or all of the cost. You may choose to approach your bank about a personal loan. Sometimes, the best option is to finance through the jeweler; some will offer a line of credit with no interest for up to a year. There is no shame in checking around to find the best deal. Consider the interest rate along with the minimum monthly payments and any escalating clauses (there might be no interest for 6 months, but after that grace period, the interest rate may skyrocket).

You do not need to include your girlfriend in these decisions. Talking to her about taking out loans for her engagement ring may diminish some of the excitement of your proposal. If she asks how much you paid (and she shouldn't), generic responses are acceptable. Feel free to use any of the following: "The money doesn't matter as long as you are happy," "Seeing the happiness in your eyes is worth any cost," or our personal favorite, "I could never put a price on my love for you."

A diamond is the traditional stone used in engagement rings. The most popular and classic shape is round. Other options include princess, emerald, oval, cushion, pear, and marquise cuts. Don't be afraid to seek other opinions when picking out the right style for her. If you don't want to ruin the surprise by asking your girlfriend, you may ask for advice from one of her close friends or relatives.

The diamond solitaire (a single stone set on a plain band) is the most traditional style for an engagement ring. In the past few years, there has been an increase in demand for antique or retro styles. These designs often have small side stones and décor around the entire ring. Remember, though a style may be trendy now—for example, the princess cut— it may not be as stylish in the future. In the 1980s, the marquise cut was the hottest style on the market, but twenty years later, very few rings of this style are being sold.

When choosing a center stone for her engagement ring, it is always best to choose a natural stone. Diamonds aren't your only choice. Some people choose sapphires or rubies. However, you should know for sure that that is what your girlfriend wants. If a diamond doesn't fit into your budget, there are alternatives, such as cubic zirconia. Again, before choosing a stone other than a diamond, it is advisable to have her approval. The last thing you want is for her to feel taken for granted. Like it or not, public perception is a large part of the engagement process. A woman will want to show off her ring to friends and family. Unless she is comfortable with the alternatives, a diamond is the way to go.

If you are concerned about the ethics surrounding the purchase of real diamonds, then you can buy stones that are mined in Canada. These diamonds are guaranteed to be conflict-free and the diamond can be traced from the mine all the way to the polished stone. Keep in mind that such stones tend to have a higher cost.

You want to make sure that the ring will fit on her finger when you propose. While most rings can be sized after the proposal, she probably will want to wear it right away, and you don't want to risk it falling off or not fitting at all. There are several ways to get a reading on her finger size.

1. Find an existing ring that she wears.
2. Explain to the jeweler her body weight and type.
3. Get advice from her friends and family.
4. Take her to get her ring finger sized (only if she knows a proposal is coming).

You'll also have your choice when it comes to engagement ring bands. White colored metals, such as white gold and platinum, are the most commonly used today. Ten years ago, yellow gold was the standard. While platinum is the most expensive, it's also the safest bet. About fifteen percent of people have allergies to the nickel alloy used in white gold. Thus, if a white metal is preferred, platinum or palladium (a soft silver/white metal with characteristics similar to platinum) are good choices. Rings can be bought on the spot or custom-made to order. It is important to speak with your jeweler regarding the necessary time to produce a custom ring.

Tip
Go with a diamond unless you're *sure* she wants a different stone.

One way to make sure your girlfriend gets a ring she'll love is to bring her along to the jewelry store. There is nothing wrong with shopping around a bit with your girlfriend. (You can always replace the surprise of the ring with an elaborate and special proposal.) You don't even have to let her pick out the specific ring in order to come up with a general idea of which types of rings she's drawn to. Before you go, you will want to set a budget for the ring. You don't want her thinking of the Rockies when you are thinking more about the sledding hill at the neighborhood park. Once again, be honest. She won't want to wear something that is embarrassingly small, but you also don't want to have to refinance your house.

3

THE RING:

A Buyer's Guide

(See images on pages 26–28)

TIPS

- Know the 4 Cs: Cut, Clarity, Color, and Carat.
- Only buy rings that have been rated by the American Gem Society (AGS) or the Gemological Institute of America (GIA).
- Be ready to compromise on purchasing a perfect diamond—you won't be able to afford one that's flawless.
- Pick out a band color that works for your girlfriend. Platinum is the most expensive and currently the

trendiest. Yellow gold is classic and the most traditional choice.

- Make sure the prongs are attached correctly, because they protect your investment in the diamond. Use the loupe to look at them closely, and do the paper test.
- Shop around to find a jeweler you can trust. This will ensure that you come away happy with your purchase.

Buying a diamond engagement ring is easy—for a diamond and setting expert. Fortunately for the rest of us, diamond experts at the Gem Institute of America (GIA) have established a rating system to assess the level of quality for each of the four most important attributes of a diamond, which they call the 4 Cs: cut, carat, clarity, and color. The

GIA is a non-profit organization dedicated to education and research about diamonds and other gems. In 1953, the GIA created the International Diamond Grading System™ (now called the 4 Cs) which is recognized throughout the world today as the standard for diamond ratings. These ratings allow you to verify the quality of the stone you are considering. Compare these ratings to the specs on a new car: Is this a 6-cylinder or 8-cylinder, 185-horsepower or 275-horsepower ring?

Even with the 4 Cs, there is potential for human error and variance. One jeweler might rate a ring differently than another. The two laboratories that are recognized as the most credible are the GIA and the American Gem Society Lab (AGSL). The American Gem Society (AGS) is a non-profit organization, similar to the GIA, established to educate and protect consumers through education and research.

Neither the AGS nor the GIA set pricing for diamonds. The market establishes the price according to the fair assessment of the labs' ratings. We recommend only buying diamonds that have been rated by the AGS or the GIA, as this will best ensure you know what you are getting.

THE FOUR Cs

Cut

The diamond's cut is what gives it the sparkle, because the cut controls how the light enters and exits the diamond. If the diamond isn't cut properly, it won't reach its maximum brilliance. It's like the engine in a car. A car can have all the bells and whistles, but without a good engine it will never perform as it should, and it won't be as valuable. Similarly, a huge diamond in an elaborate setting is practically worthless if it's not cut well.

Diamonds do not leave the mines in a condition suitable for use in fine jewelry. It takes a diamond cutter to cut them into different shapes:

round, oval, marquise, pear, emerald-cut, princess-cut, or cushion-cut. All these shapes are acceptable choices in engagement rings. While the shape affects the cut, it does not affect the quality or classification of the cut. Do not confuse the shape with a diamond's cut quality.

Because the cut of a diamond is considered the most important aspect of the gem, there are four classifications of cut quality: ideal, fine, shallow, and deep. A diamond that has an ideal cut is just that—ideal. It has been cut to the right proportions. You will be able to see reflected white light, called brilliance. The rainbow of colors you see—sometimes called fire, technically known as dispersion—is the breaking up of white light into colors. In an ideal cut, the light is captured through the table and shines on the pavilion, which reflects the light back through the table to create the perfect brilliance and sparkle.

Fine-cut diamonds are considered well-cut diamonds. Although not perfect, they will correctly reflect the majority of light. This is a great option when you are trying to reduce some of the expense of a diamond without sacrificing much quality.

Shallow-cut diamonds are diamonds that do not have a long enough pavilion. This is a problem; when the light is captured through the diamond's table, it shines to the pavilion. Instead of reflecting back through the table, light leaks out of the bottom, decreasing brilliance.

Deep-cut diamonds are just the opposite. The pavilion is too long, which causes the light to escape through the sides of the diamond. Again, this depletes the diamond's brilliance and sparkle. Often a diamond is deep cut because a cutter is trying to retain the diamond's carat weight. Leaving space in the pavilion is an easy way for a diamond to have a larger carat weight, but it will negatively affect its brilliance and sparkle. The reason that a diamond would be deep-cut is because uneducated buyers often buy on the carat weight alone, and this cut is an easy way for jewelers to make a higher profit.

Tip

Do not confuse the shape with a diamond's cut quality.

Remember While Shopping

Do not confuse the shape of the diamond with the cut. The cut is very different and is what creates the brilliance, scintillation, and dispersion in the ring. A diamond with an ideal cut will shine with both white and fire colors, while one without the right cut will reflect little more than any other gem.

Carat

The term carat refers to the actual weight of the stone. It is easy to think the bigger the better, but carat weight alone does not determine the value of a gem. Even educated buyers will ask you and your fiancée how big the ring is once they see it on her finger, making it feel more important than other considerations. But remember, carat is just one of the 4 Cs.

On page 26 you can find a scale of diamonds that shows the actual size of a .25 carat-weight diamond on up to a 5 carat-weight diamond to help you begin to choose the stone size that you would like to purchase. Once you have chosen a carat size, look for pricing compatible with the optimum quality of the remaining Cs you desire. Then decide if you should increase or reduce the carat weight in order to stay within your price range while maintaining your cut, clarity, and color preferences.

Clarity

Clarity is the third "C" to be considered when buying a diamond. Clarity refers to relative freedom from blemishes. It is rare to find a diamond without any imperfections at all. Flaws refer to imperfections on the surface of the diamond, while inclusions are the imperfections in the body of the diamond. Cutters try to remove all the flaws possible by buffing the stone, but inclusions are impossible to move. Inclusions are created when non-diamond crystals are trapped inside the diamond while it is forming.

Inclusions limit the ability of light to pass through the diamond. Again, it is very rare to find a diamond without any inclusions, but try to choose a gem with inclusions that are invisible to the naked eye. Inclusions look whitish and have grainy, crystal, or line appearances when light reflects on the gem.

What would a flaw and inclusion look like on your car? Flaws would be the number of surface nicks, scratches, or dings. Inclusions are more like rust that forms under your paint, which you won't be able to remove. When you wax the car, those marks just won't shine the way you want them to.

There is a clarity rating scale for lab-rated diamonds. It ranges from flawless to imperfect. You can find a diamond clarity scale on page 26. Below is a written description of the scale. Remember, gemologists are trained to rate diamonds, so do not think that you will be able to walk into a diamond store and know the value of a diamond just by looking at it.

> **Remember While Shopping**
>
> Do not overemphasize the importance of the carat weight. It is important not to let a jeweler sell you a ring based only on the size of the gem. Know that just because a diamond is larger it does not mean it is more valuable—unless the other three Cs are of great value as well.

Remember While Shopping

Clarity, like cut, can affect the way your diamond sparkles and the way light shines when it hits the gem. Buy a lab-rated diamond so you can know that a trained professional has inspected the diamond that you are buying. Do not try to rate the diamond's clarity on your own or with a jeweler you do not trust, because you will miss inclusions both with the naked eye and under a microscope. Know the scale for a lab-certified diamond.

FL—Flawless: No internal or external inclusions when viewed under a 10x microscope.

IF—Internally Flawless: No internal inclusions, but contains slight surface blemishes that cannot be removed with polishing.

VVS1—Very, Very Slightly Included 1: Insignificant inclusions, such as reflective internal graining, difficult to see using a 10x microscope.

VVS2—Very, Very Slightly Included 2: Minute inclusions less difficult to see using a 10x microscope than a VVS1 gem.

VS1—Very Slightly Included 1: Small inclusions visible under a 10x microscope.

VS2—Very Slightly Included 2: Slightly easier to see small inclusions under a 10x microscope than VS1.

SI1—Slightly Included 1: Inclusions easily seen under a 10x microscope.

SI2—Slightly Included 2: Inclusions are very easy to see and locate under a 10x microscope.

I1—Imperfect 1: Inclusions are visible with the naked eye and are very obvious under a 10x microscope.

I2—Imperfect 2: Inclusions are visible with the naked eye and may interfere with the transparency and brilliance.

I3—Imperfect 3: Dark inclusions are noticeable to the naked eye and interfere with transparency. This grade is likely to worsen with wear as well.

Color

Color is the fourth "C" to consider when buying a diamond. There is a scale of measurement to follow for this as well. While there are actually more than 300 known colors of diamonds found in nature, the scale we will talk about is for the "white or colorless" diamonds. These are the most common diamonds and the most often used in an engagement ring. Diamonds that have a color other than clear are called "fancy colors" and demand top dollar. As for white diamonds, the goal is to purchase one that is entirely colorless. These diamonds will best reflect light, create brilliance, and shine. Lab-rated diamonds have a scale from "D" to "Z." Stones are rated apart from the settings and in very specific light. Outside colors, such as a jewelry setting, can easily influence the actual diamond color, which will create an inaccurate rating. A white diamond's color is often influenced by nitrogen while it is forming, which creates a yellow look to the diamond.

When buying a traditional white diamond, depending on your price range, it is wise to choose a rating between D and M: "D" is a perfectly colorless diamond, "M" is considered a faint yellow diamond, and "Z" is a full, fancy-colored yellow. Any color rating above H should appear colorless to the natural untrained eye.

Remember While Shopping

When purchasing a white diamond, it should be as close to colorless as possible. The more yellow it is, the less your diamond will shine. If the diamond is already in a setting, you or the jeweler cannot assign any color rating, as this feature can only be determined for loose diamonds. Look for diamonds that have been lab rated.

THE SETTING AND THE BAND

The setting and band on a diamond ring add the finishing touches. There are numerous settings to choose from, and designers constantly create their own as well. The first thing to decide is what precious metal you will use for the setting and band. Generally, the band and the setting will be a fraction of the total cost of a diamond ring, and these components will protect the diamond from falling out and getting lost. Do not nickel and dime the setting, as you might regret it later.

The main options for settings are gold, white gold, and platinum. Some jewelers offer to have the setting plated with these metals to reduce the cost, but keep in mind that the plating will wear away, creating space between the diamond and the prongs, which makes it easier for the diamond to fall out. (Plating means using a thin layer of the metal you want over a cheaper metal to create the look you want without the expense.) According to fashion, one of these three metals can seem to be more popular than the other two, but in reality, it is you and your soon-to-be-bride's personal preference that should determine which metal you choose. No, you do not need to ask her; you can tell generally if she prefers gold or silver jewelry by observing the jewelry she already wears.

Right now, platinum is rising in popularity. Platinum is the strongest and purest metal used by jewelers. It will not wear or tarnish and is resistant to damage. It is rarer than gold, which means that it is the most expensive option. The price of platinum is usually almost twice the price of gold, depending on its availability.

White gold is often used as a substitute for platinum. It is a gold alloy, which means it is gold combined with platinum, nickel, zinc, and/or palladium. This combination gives it the silver or platinum appearance. If white gold is not of high quality, it will not retain its shine well. Because of this, many white gold alloys are coated with rhodium in order to give it a shine that is comparable to silver or platinum. The rhodium is likely to wear away over time and will need to be replaced. Be aware that some people have an allergic reaction to white gold due to its nickel content.

Yellow gold is the all-time most popular setting choice for diamond engagement rings. It is the most malleable metal known, which is why it is used so widely in jewelry. When purchasing a gold setting and band, you choose what karat level of gold you want. Karat is the term used to measure the purity of the gold. Gold that is less than 24 karats is part silver, copper, nickel, and zinc.

- 12-karat gold is 50 percent pure
- 18-karat gold is 75 percent pure
- 24-karat gold is 99.99 percent pure and is considered fully pure by industry standards

Higher karat gold is shinier, considered more precious, and is also more expensive. 24-karat is too soft for rings. 18-karat is considered best suited for an engagement ring, and as low as 14-karat can be used.

THE PRONGS

Prongs are the part of the setting that actually come in contact with the diamond and secure the stone to the band. Carefully inspecting the prongs is very important. This is what actually holds the diamond in place. If the prongs are not secured, it is possible that the diamond could fall out. The easiest test to ensure the prongs are on securely is to take a piece of paper and try to slip it under the prongs. If the paper fits between any of the prongs and the diamond, it is not secure enough. Demand that the problem with the prongs be corrected before you take the ring home.

The number of prongs on the ring will vary depending on the shape of the diamond you choose. The thing to look for no matter how many prongs is that they are evenly spaced on the diamond.

GENERAL BUYING TIPS

Know the rating systems before you pick out your ring. You don't need to memorize everything, but have a good understanding of each of the scales. Think about which of the 4 Cs you are willing to compromise on before you go to the jewelry store. Decide for yourself what level of each C you are looking to purchase, knowing that trying for perfection in all 4 Cs is going to be very expensive. Once you set the parameters for the quality of the ring you want, consider which one or two areas you could adjust as needed when you are actually at the jewelers. Having a feel for what you want and how much you are willing to compromise on diamond quality will help ensure that you are not "sold" on a diamond, but that you choose the engagement ring you want.

When you are presented with individual diamond stones, ask for the jeweler's loupe. The loupe is the instrument a jeweler uses to examine the diamond quality. Again, you are not an expert, so don't expect to use the loupe to assign your own rating to each one of the Cs. However, this will help you notice some obvious flaws in the diamond. When you use the loupe, ask the jeweler what blemishes you should see in each specific diamond. A helpful, honest jeweler should have no problem pointing out the flaws because they know that unless you are Donald Trump, you aren't going to buy one that is perfect! Use the loupe to examine the setting as well. Make sure the prongs are in contact with the diamond.

If you are presented with a number of loose diamonds and one very obviously stands out as better than the others, be wary. Stacking the deck in one stone's favor may cause the buyer to think that diamond is of higher quality or has more value than it really does. Ask to view a diamond with stones of similar quality and compare their professional ratings, as well as their visual appeal, to avoid being pushed into an impulse purchase.

Another thing to be leery of is buying a lab-certified diamond that is not certified by either the AGS or the GIA. These two labs exist to protect the consumer and set the industry standard for fairly rating diamonds in the United States. When you buy an AGS or GIA lab-certified diamond, paperwork is provided with the official certification. Some jewelers will claim to have machines or other methods to certify their own diamonds. Avoid buying a diamond from such a jeweler because they may have inflated ratings generated by unreliable rating standards or questionably calibrated private machines.

Buying an engagement ring will be one of the most important things you do in the engagement process, so be sure to do your research ahead of time. Remember, use the rating systems and look for the ring that meets your requirements, as you would when buying a car. Having an understanding of what you are looking for ahead of time will help you feel more comfortable when you are at the jeweler's. Find a jeweler you can trust. If you can trust your jeweler, and you have an idea of what you want going into the store, you will have the tools you need to select a beautiful engagement ring for your special lady.

	0.25ct	0.50ct	0.75ct	1.00ct	1.50ct	2.00ct
	4.1mm	5.2mm	5.9mm	6.5mm	7.4mm	8.2mm

CARAT SCALE

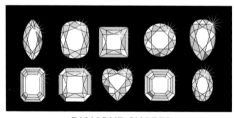

GIA	FL-IF	VVS1-VVS2	VS1-VS2	SI1-SI2	I1-I2-I3
AGS	0-1	2-3	4-5	6-7	8-9-10
Clarity Grading Diagram	Internally Flawless	Very Very Slight Inclusions	Very Slight Inclusions	Slight Inclusions	Imperfect

DIAMOND CLARITY SCALE

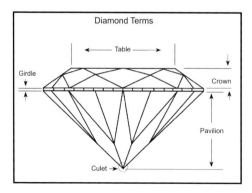

DIAMOND SHAPES

TOP: MARQUISE, CUSHION, PRINCESS, ROUND, PEAR
BOTTOM: EMERALD, RADIANT, HEART, ASSCHER, OVAL

Diamond Terms

Table

Girdle

Crown

Pavilion

Culet

DIAMOND TERMS

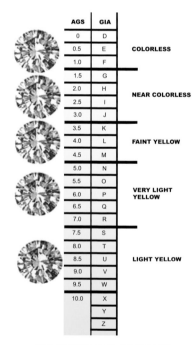

AGS	GIA	
0	D	COLORLESS
0.5	E	
1.0	F	
1.5	G	NEAR COLORLESS
2.0	H	
2.5	I	
3.0	J	
3.5	K	FAINT YELLOW
4.0	L	
4.5	M	
5.0	N	
5.5	O	VERY LIGHT YELLOW
6.0	P	
6.5	Q	
7.0	R	
7.5	S	
8.0	T	LIGHT YELLOW
8.5	U	
9.0	V	
9.5	W	
10.0	X	
	Y	
	Z	

DIAMOND COLOR SCALE

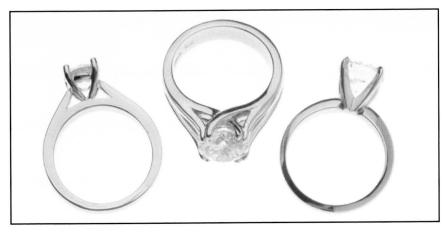

YELLOW GOLD (LEFT), PLATINUM (CENTER), AND WHITE GOLD (RIGHT)

PRINCESS CUT DIAMOND

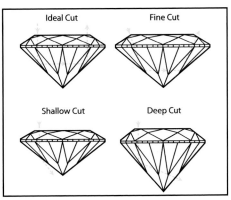

DIAMOND CUTS AND LIGHT REFLECTION

PRONGS

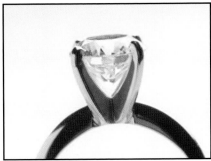

PRONGS—SIDE VIEW

PRONGS—TOP VIEW

CLASSIC SOLITAIRE SETTING

SOLITAIRE CATHEDRAL SETTING

SOLITAIRE TRELLIS SETTING

PART TWO

REAL PROPOSALS

4

RULES OF ENGAGEMENT:
How to propose like a pro so you don't get shot down

In the popular Joaquin Phoenix and Reese Witherspoon movie *Walk the Line*, the Johnny Cash character repeatedly proposes to June Carter, only to get shot down every time. Cash says, "I've asked you forty different ways, and it's time you come up with a fresh answer."

But before June finally gives him the answer he wants to hear, she gives him a few pointers on how *not* to propose to a woman. For instance: "Don't propose to a woman when you're drunk; don't tell her it's because you've had a bad dream; and never propose to a girl on a bus."

If you're considering asking the woman of your dreams to marry you, and you're willing to "walk the line," you need to think about your approach, too–about how, when, and where you should propose. That's why, in the next several chapters, we offer true-life stories of how other grooms have done it to give you a bit of inspiration and hope, as well as some advice arising from hard-earned experience on what *not* to do.

So, before you choose which way you're going to pop the question, it's good to consider some of the rules of engagement. June's rules in *Walk the Line* still apply today, for her words hint at a greater truth than most guys have ever even considered: There are some definite rules to which you must adhere–rules about how these things are done and about what women expect. And, be aware–your girlfriend knows the rules, even if you don't.

GET SERIOUS

RULE ONE: *You've got to be sober—*

and no, not just literally (it's a no-brainer that you should never get drunk and ask a girl to marry you—we trust you're well beyond that stage). No, what this rule really means is that you've got to take this whole thing very seriously. You've got to know, absolutely, what you're doing and what you're both feeling. You've got to be sure this woman is truly the one for you. You've got to carefully plan not only the proposal, but the rest of your life—what you and she both expect from marriage.

RULE TWO: *Don't be in love with love—*

or simply buy into the "dream." You're about to ask a woman to marry you. This is the real thing. Don't propose on a whim. Don't propose because you're scared of being alone or you had a bad dream. Don't propose because it sounds like a good idea, or you think it may bring back the "sparks" or fan a "flame" that seems to be going out in the relationship. Propose because you can't take one more breath, can't live one more moment, unless she's part of it. Propose because you're ready to walk the line and be faithful to one woman, alone—forever.

THE IMPORTANCE OF PLACE

RULE THREE: *Proposals are like nouns.*

They're about the person, place, and the thing—and, yes, the place part matters. You've got to do the proposing in the *right* place at the *right* time. No, not the place *you* think is right, or even necessarily the time you think is right. It's got to be her right place, her right time—the place she would pick if she were dreaming about a marriage proposal, at the exact moment she's ready to hear those four little words, "Will you marry me?"

Remember, you're asking her for something pretty wonderful, mind-blowingly special, and completely life-changing. You're trying to convince her that you care more about her than life itself. If your proposal occurs in a place she doesn't like, at a time when she's not ready, or if it is done in a way that is all about you and not about her, that tells her something "not great" about what her life is going to be like if she says, "Yes."

> Remember, you're asking her for something pretty wonderful, mind-blowingly special, and completely life-changing. You're trying to convince her that you care more about her than life itself.

THIS IS ABOUT HER

RULE FOUR: *This isn't just about you.*

In fact, most women think the proposal, engagement, and wedding are mostly about her–the bride.

If you want your prospective bride to say yes and years later to still be gushing about how you proposed to her, pay attention to what she wants, what she'd like, what she's been dreaming of (yes, women have been talking and dreaming about this since the world's first slumber party). So try to come up with a proposal that tells her you know her well and you've thought about what she'd like, not just what you'd like. Don't take her to a hockey game and put "Marry me" on the score board if she hates hockey, even if

> The proposal window is a small and fragile one, because you have got to both be sure at the same time that you want the same thing, forever.

you love it. Has she been trying to drag you to the ballet? Has she always wanted to go to that fancy restaurant that you never want to try? That's it. You're getting warmer.

TAKE YOUR TIME

RULE FIVE: *Take all the time you need.*

How long have you been together? If the answer is considerably less than a year, it's very likely that the time isn't right. Forever takes a long time, and so it deserves more consideration than you may be giving it. You should know for sure that this one is a keeper and you're not going to trade her for next year's model. It's a tricky thing, though–there's a fine line between waiting until you know one another well enough and waiting too long. The proposal window is a small and fragile one, because you have got to both be sure at the same time that you want the same thing, forever.

RULE SIX: *Don't take too long.*

True, "You Can't Hurry Love," as the old song goes, but you don't want her theme song to be "Stop Dragging My Heart Around," either. Don't let proposing go so long that the woman you love turns into a lunatic who constantly nags about when you two are going to get married, or cries on the phone to her girlfriends that you are never going to commit, and all the while her biological clock is ticking. Under a year is probably not long enough. Assuming you're both old enough to have lived on your own at least a few years and established yourselves in your careers and in your lives as individuals, at the one-year mark, take a good look at the situation. As you approach the first-year anniversary, maybe a month or two beforehand, if you don't have to ask yourself if she's the one because you already know, and you know she knows, too, then the time may be right . . . provided you two are as much in sync as you think you are.

As for the biological clock business: If you want kids someday, but the idea of starting right now frightens you, we understand. However, you also need to understand and be mature enough to face the realization that "someday" has an expiration date, not only for her, but for you. If this is indeed the woman that you know should be the mother of your children, don't wait until it is too late for her to have kids or until she leaves you to start a family with someone else. She can't wait forever, and if you love her, she shouldn't have to.

FAILURE TO LAUNCH

RULE SEVEN: *Remember—there's no such thing as fear of commitment.*

If you fear you can't commit, maybe it's because part of you doesn't want to. If you don't want to, there's a reason for that. Pay attention to that reason.

RULE EIGHT: *Beware the Ides of March, or the 14th of February, or the 25th of December.*

If your girlfriend is pushing for a ring because it's almost Valentine's Day or Christmas Eve, step away from the girlfriend. That's not to say you can't *ever* give a woman an engagement ring under the mistletoe or with

> You want to get married because you're sure—not just because it is sentimental or "expected."

a heart-shaped box of chocolates. But if there's one molecule of your being that senses that her time frame has more to do with a Hallmark holiday than with how she feels about you, about forever, and about growing old together, do not even consider giving her a ring right now. Yes, she may be the one, she may be the future mother of your children, and she may love you madly, truly, deeply. But then again she may just be someone who puts more stock in sentiment than in deep and lasting love. Be sure this is what you want and not just what she wants, when she wants. You want to get married because you're sure—not just because it is sentimental or "expected," even if you know she's got her heart set on a Christmas ring. Remember, while the rules above state that this is about her, don't kid yourself—we know that it is just as much about you: your timing, your dreams, your gut feeling as to when the time is right.

This is your life. Don't screw it up.

RULE NINE: *Don't let her pressure you.*

If a woman has been pressuring you to get married and you're not entirely against the idea, but part of you isn't that thrilled about it either, don't propose just yet. Or if you're reading this book because a woman wants you to and you are just going through the motions because you don't want to hurt her feelings or you don't want to wake up lonely tomorrow, it may be time to end—or rethink—the relationship. Don't hang on when it's over. Don't drag out the breakup if it is bound to come later. That not only wastes everyone's time, it is more painful that way. So pull off that Band-Aid quickly. As the Paul Simon song says, "Slip out the back, Jack. Make a new plan, Stan. Don't need to be coy, Roy. Just set yourself free."

RULE TEN: *This is about you.*

There are so few things in life that you get to decide for yourself and that are 100 percent your own, and, man, marriage is one of them. Your life is yours alone. You only get one shot at it. So you have to decide what is right for you—just you—not her. Here's the thing: She gets to decide what is right for her; you get to decide for you. She can know you inside out, from how you take your coffee to the password on your e-mail, to the name of the first dog you ever had, but she can't know *for* you or decide *for* you that she's "the one." When it comes to knowing that, you're not only allowed to be entirely selfish, you *must* be. You have an obligation to yourself to take care of your life, your heart, and your future—even if it means you're going to hurt a really great woman, and even if it means you have to feel lonely and hurt for a while, too.

> You have an obligation to yourself to take care of your life, your heart, and your future—even if it means you're going to hurt a really great woman, and even if it means you have to feel lonely and hurt for a while, too.

RULE ELEVEN: *If you aren't dying to marry her—and I mean D-Y-I-N-G to marry her—then don't—*

because if you marry her anyway, there's a strong chance that you're going to shrivel up and die inside emotionally, and that's the kind of dying that you won't get over so quickly—neither will she, nor the kids you may have by then.

Don't go into marriage with low expectations. Don't go through life with low expectations for yourself. Respect and love yourself, and her, enough to want the very best for one another . . . even if that means the very best thing or person for each of you may be someone else, somewhere down the line.

RULE TWELVE: *Only ask if you're sure she's going to say yes.*

Yes, you'd think this is stating the obvious, but you'd be surprised how many guys forget this rule and end up with a stupid look on their face and a horrible ache in their hearts. If you have to ask to know if she wants to marry you, you probably shouldn't. If you know she wants to marry you, without her even having to say a word, then, buddy, the time is right.

RULE THIRTEEN: *Ask her daddy.*

Or mother. Or brother. Or whomever it is that she'd want you to ask. Just do it. Unless the family dynamic is such that it's clearly inappropriate to do so, it's almost always a good idea. She'll adore you for doing this, we promise.

RULE FOURTEEN: *Diamonds are a guy's best friend.*

Get a ring. Even if it is a Cracker Jack box ring that will have to do until she picks out the one she wants, don't leave home without one. Unless you give her a ring at that moment, part of her will always think it's not a "real" proposal. Some women don't like diamonds (not many, assuredly, but some don't). Others have a certain carat requirement. One prominent Austin, Texas, attorney advises, "Never propose to a woman with a diamond that's less than 2 carats: there's not a woman alive who will say no to that." The rule of thumb in the jewelry industry is that an engagement ring should cost you the equivalent of two month's salary, but what else would you expect a jeweler to say? Spend less? So forget that and remember this: Don't get yourself in debt. Don't spend beyond your means. If she loves you, she won't want you to start off married life saddled with debt. Buy what you can afford, but first study rings carefully and learn about how to recognize a quality diamond. If at all possible, make the choice together. The bride has to like the ring; after all, she's going to wear it every day for the rest of her life. If you still have questions on this topic perhaps you should spend a little more time on the previous chapters.

> Don't get yourself in debt. Don't spend beyond your means. If she loves you, she won't want to start off married life saddled with debt.

We interviewed a woman who was wearing an engagement ring that she really doesn't like. Getting it was a big disappointment because it was not at all the kind of ring she'd always imagined. Ten years later she's still wearing it with her wedding band, and she still doesn't like it. It took a bit of the sparkle off the happiness of the moment when she felt she had to pretend she was happy with the ring when he proposed.

With the right ring, your lady love is sure to sparkle at that special moment when she knows that you know that she's the one.

RULE FIFTEEN: *The last rule is—there are no rules.*

If none of the above rules seem to apply to you—you've searched your soul and know that this is right—and if you're sure you *both* are equally sure, even if your relationship doesn't fit some of the rules of engagement outlined above, then you have our permission to ignore it all. Go for it. It's time to propose!

Now that you're sober (serious) and you're in the right place (emotionally, spiritually, and physically) to get married, all you have to do is figure out how and when to propose. You'll want to create a perfect moment that neither of you will ever forget.

READY, SET, GO

Feeling the pressure? Sure. But can you handle it? Yeah–because we're here to help. In the following chapters we'll give you ideas for how to propose to the woman you love and ways that worked for other guys–today's grooms who applied the rules of engagement and got shot down only by cupid's arrows.

Oh, and there's one more rule that can't be broken: You have to sweep her off her feet.

· 5 ·

THE TRADITIONALIST

The traditional proposal is usually made in a romantic setting—perhaps at a tiny table in the back of a dark restaurant, or in a fabulous hotel lobby, or on the steps of a church after a wedding. Perhaps it takes place during a moonlit walk on the beach, or at the place where you two first met. It's an unwritten rule that the prospective bridegroom should already have the ring, and always, in a traditional engagement, he's required to get down on one knee to ask the woman he loves to be his wife.

Although some may say there's nothing particularly novel about this approach, the great thing is that this method never goes out of style. A woman in love will almost always cry with joy when she sees the man she loves on bended knee with a ring. If you have a beautiful diamond on hand, she'll know you mean business, and it will be even more special. If you want to wait until she picks out the ring, that's fine too, but have a token ring you can give her at that moment and then tell her that she'll get to pick out the real one herself.

Remember: To be truly traditional, you should ask her father or family for permission beforehand, though these days that's usually just a respectful formality that makes the woman swoon and that the family appreciates.

Here are a few stories of real-life proposals from men that took the traditional route.

MOVE OVER, BRIDE AND GROOM

This groom-to-be used someone else's wedding photo op to set up his marriage proposal at the Four Seasons Hotel in Atlanta, Georgia

Chip Knickerbockers shares his story . . .

My mom always told me that if I were going to propose, I'd need to make it a special day for the lucky girl. On April 22, 2006, the woman I love, Kristin Green, got to find out how special that proposal could be.

Kristin and I had plans for dinner and a night on the town with some friends. Kristin thought that she had planned the whole evening, but little did she know I had her friends set her up.

Before our date, I told her I was taking the car out to get it washed, but really I went to pick up her ring and called her brother and dad to ask for their permission to marry Kristin. After that, I washed the car and then picked her up for her first surprise.

Seeing how it was warm out and that she was wearing sandals a lot, I thought it would be a nice treat for her to get a pedicure. Then, just when she thought that we were done with the surprise, we walked into a special salon to get massages. Afterwards, we went home to get ready to meet our friends for the night. We arranged to meet another couple, Will and Kate, at the Four Seasons Hotel in midtown Atlanta for a pre-dinner drink.

At this point I was so anxious that I was fidgeting a good bit. I had planned on popping the question as soon as we walked in, while standing on the beautiful marble staircase in the lobby. But, as luck would have it, there was a wedding party taking pictures on the staircase right at that moment. So we used

> **Tip**
> A hitch in the plans doesn't have to ruin your moment. Be creative. Things may turn out better than you'd imagined.

the elevator to get up to the lounge as I tried to come up with a Plan B. Hearing of my dilemma, Will decided to ask the wedding party how long they were going to take. He explained to them why I needed the staircase and they answered happily that they'd be gone shortly.

We finished our drinks and started to leave the hotel. When we got to the steps, I asked Kate to take a picture of us. As she was doing this, she asked me when I was going to make Kristin a bride like the one whom we'd just seen earlier taking photographs on the stairs.

When Kristin was done blushing, I got down on one knee and asked her to marry me. After she said yes, we got a loud round of applause. We had no idea that the bridal party that had been on the stairs stayed to watch me in action.

—

THE WOMAN OF HIS DREAMS

This couple met in their dreams years before they met on the Internet

This proposal story comes from a bride and groom whose engagement really was a dream come true. (Maybe June was wrong in the movie when she told Johnny Cash not to tell a girl you're proposing because of a dream you had.) This story is magical and still has that traditional touch of a romantic place and a sparkling ring. In this story, the bride, Elizabeth, tells about the dreams and the dream proposal that would forever change her life.

Elizabeth Bechtel of Eden Prairie, Minnesota, first told this story to "The Diamond Guy" —famed author and diamond expert Fred Cuellar— who related the story to us because it was so incredible. Cuellar is the author of three books: *How to Buy a Diamond, Diamonds for Profit,* and *World's Greatest Proposal Stories.*

"When he sent me his pictures, I recognized his face from my dream. I know that sounds crazy, but it's true. I still had the drawing from before, and I knew it was him."

I was in the third grade when I had a rather memorable dream. In it, I had wandered into another country. There were ruins of ancient walls, and children were flying kites. A single kite broke loose from its string and wafted toward me as all the children laughed. I joined the group of kite-flyers, and we had a wonderful time, until I wanted to go home. I asked the other children to show me the way home because I was lost, but nobody would help me—except one little boy.

The boy guided me on a long journey until we neared a place I recognized as a park near my house. There was a wooden bridge that cut through the middle of the park across a small river, and I expected the boy would come with me. But just as we reached the bridge, the boy said that he had to leave.

As he stood on one side of the bridge, I begged the boy to come and cross with me. I had so much to show him—my house, my family, my cat—just on the other side. But the boy said that he could not come now. He promised someday he would.

When I awoke, I told my parents about the dream. It was so vivid. As I explained the dream to my parents, I drew a picture of the kites and the boy.

Years passed, and I met a guy named Jay on the Internet. When he sent me his pictures, I recognized his face from my dream.

I know that sounds crazy, but it's true. I still had the drawing from before, and I knew it was him. But I decided not to tell him this, lest I sound too strange.

Jay and I began e-mailing each other several times a day, and after some time, we began talking on the phone all night. Although we had to go to work without sleeping, we felt wonderful!

I was scheduled for vacation and had tickets to fly to Cancun, Mexico, with my Mom, when Jay asked if I could re-route my plans and come meet him instead. While my Mom basked on Cancun's beaches, I was visiting the cornfields of Indiana, but I had no regrets.

Jay met me at the airport with pink roses, took me to meet his friends, and showed me the tourist spots. We talked for days at a time. When my vacation began nearing an end, he brought me to see his apartment. I could not imagine why he would want me to see his apartment (except perhaps to demonstrate that it was neat and clean), but he was insistent.

Since he was a graduate student, he shared the apartment with two roommates, but both of them were absent.

"I should wait for the guys," he muttered to himself. I did not know why we were waiting for his roommates, or what for, nor would he tell me. After we had waited for perhaps half an hour, Jay suggested we take a walk.

It was dusk, and the sky was purple. We walked to a bridge; the water below was inky and seemed to sparkle in the twilight. Jay began to glance nervously around, and then he started reciting my favorite Shakespearian sonnet (#65), ". . . that in black ink my love might still shine bright."

After he finished reciting the poem, he got down on one knee, took a silver band off of his own hand and proposed to me.

I said, "Yes."

The two of us crossed the bridge together and returned to his apartment. There, he gave me a bag full of presents to unwrap, placed a pearl necklace around my neck, and fed me sweets.

Just as my mouth was full of candy, his friends, roommates, and a friend's girlfriend arrived.

"We're too late!" the girlfriend exclaimed, noticing the pearls around my neck. "Oh my gosh, we missed the proposal! He's proposed already without us!"

It turned out that Jay had planned a public proposal with all his friends present, but had brushed it aside on the spur of a moment, to propose to me alone at the bridge.

The story might have ended there, but on our wedding night, Jay told me how nervous he had been.

He said, "I didn't want to tell you this until after the wedding because you might think I'm weird, but when I was a kid, I dreamed about flying a kite with a little girl, and she looked just like you!"

THE SECOND TIME AROUND

Love is sweeter (and the proposal more carefully planned)
the second time around.

John Sternal, the managing director of the Max Borges Agency, a successful Miami public relations firm, called us with this romantic, traditional story about his proposal to Chrisanne Dagit. He also reiterated some good advice that echoed our own, shared earlier in this book—reminding grooms of our rules that, one, this is about her and what she likes; two, this is about the two of you and forever; and three, this is an important moment in life that should be carefully considered and thoughtfully planned.

"A guy shouldn't propose on a whim. He should pay attention to details, things the woman says, things she likes, colors she loves, flowers she loves, places she loves, and make a mental note of all this. This is an important moment in your life that you'll both remember forever, so it deserves a lot of thought and planning. I spent maybe five months preparing for the proposal," says Sternal. He admits that the first time he proposed to a woman years before, he did it all wrong. He didn't really put any thought into it, and he didn't pay attention to what was important to her.

Careful to learn from his mistakes, John decided this time he'd found "the one" for him, and he was going to honor that woman and respect and cherish her enough to take time and do it correctly. A month beforehand, he went to his girlfriend's father and asked his permission to marry his daughter. Then he waited until the time was right—a time when he knew his true love would truly be surprised, and all his months of preparation would culminate in a special proposal that she would remember all her life.

The groom-to-be writes . . .

Having been married once before, I knew I wanted to make the right impression for a proposal this time around, now that I found a girl who's a much better fit for me. (Oh, the wonders of experience!)

Our entire relationship has been built on surprises (part practical joke/part nice gestures). I knew that my fiancée, Chrisanne,

> "A guy shouldn't propose on a whim. He should pay attention to details, things the woman says, things she likes, colors she loves, flowers she loves, places she loves, and make a mental note of all this...."

was sort of hoping that a proposal would be forthcoming during holiday season. But, thinking that would be too cliché, I decided to wait it out–sort of. Thanksgiving came, and no proposal. Christmas came and no proposal. New Year's Eve was upon us. I knew we would be hanging out with her good girlfriends on New Year's Eve (which fell on a Sunday night that year). So I planned to propose the night before, on that Saturday night, so that we could have the best of both worlds (a quiet night for us that Saturday night, and an opportunity for her to show off in front of her girlfriends the very next night during New Year's Eve celebrations).

Obviously, lots of planning went into this.

As the weekend approached, I informed her that we would be dining with an important client of mine who would be coming into town for the weekend. This ensured that we would have an excuse for dressing up without her having the option of backing out at the last minute from being tired or whatever.

That Saturday night came, we got all dressed up, and we proceeded to go to the Riverside Hotel, a rather famous and very special landmark hotel in Fort Lauderdale. In fact, it's the oldest hotel in the city, and better yet, it is the place where Chrisanne and I had our first kiss.

While we were in the bar having a drink, I received a (fake) phone call on my cell phone. It was supposedly my boss advising me that everyone was up in my client's suite. He urged us to come up for a drink before heading out to dinner.

So we did; well, sort of. Earlier in the day, I had arranged for us to have our own corner balcony suite at the hotel. So I made it over to the hotel without Chrisanne knowing it, and picked up the keys to the room ahead of time.

On our way up to the suite, which was ostensibly my client's room, I finally began to feel the nerves twitch and the blood rush through my veins. It was pretty cool, I must admit. Everything began to rush harder as we got closer to the door. When we did, I quickly opened the door of the completely dark room.

Chrisanne grew immediately suspicious and was confused. I knew I was on the clock and needed to do this *now*.

I took her out onto the balcony overlooking the lights of South Florida, and I popped the question. Chrisanne began to get teary-eyed, knowing that I had given her the surprise of a lifetime. She truly had absolutely no idea this would happen on this night in this way.

Naturally, she said yes (although she was so surprised she doesn't remember a word I said).

She had seen a setting for a ring that she loved a while back in a magazine and showed it to me. I'd made a note of that and sent it later to a St. Petersburg, Florida, jeweler friend of mine to have them make one just like it. The ring I had for the proposal was exactly what she wanted and much more than she ever expected. She was so surprised and shocked after I proposed that I finally had to ask her if she was ever going to even look at her ring. She was so thrilled and couldn't believe I'd had it made even bigger and better than she'd dreamed.

A December wedding is now in the planning stages, and we're both so very happy.

My advice to other guys out there is this: plan, plan, plan, and then do more planning to make sure you've thought of everything. Be sure to think of the details. If she likes a certain color, incorporate that color into that moment. If you had your first kiss somewhere, bring her back to that place. Make it meaningful and filled with details that either she likes, or that recalls something that is important to just the two of you. And above anything else, make it the biggest surprise of her life. I also can't imagine proposing without a ring. You have to have a ring, so make sure it is the one she wants.

If the traditional, romantic method is the style that's right for you and your prospective bride, you can't go wrong with a simple ring and a bended knee after you've been bestowed the blessing of her parents. But if you're a "live on the edge" kind of person who wants something a bit more extreme, read on.

6

THE EXTREMIST
Out-of-this-World Proposals

S ome couples have terribly high expectations about marriage and even higher expectations about how the proposal should go. The following stories are from grooms who followed our above rules and broke the ordinary rules, to make sure their proposals were thoughtfully planned, meticulously orchestrated, and truly unforgettable.

And unforgettable these stories are—the extremist wants his proposal to be spectacular. It takes a lot of planning and preparation to pull off a unique and exciting scenario for the proposal moment. Some want to pop the question in a hot air balloon; others want to tell the world about their love, so they put it on billboards or hire a skywriter to spell it out for them. One wild and crazy guy we know of set himself on fire—literally.

Whichever way you decide to do it, the extreme proposal is one that neither of you (or anyone who hears the story) is likely to forget. Here are some real life stories of grooms that didn't take the easy way out when it came time to ask that special woman that special question in a truly special way.

"COME ON BABY, LIGHT MY FIRE"

This is an actual *Ripley's Believe It or Not* proposal

Our next real-life proposal story comes from Oregon, where groom-to-be Todd Grannis and his lady love, Malissa Kusiek, shared a proposal that will forever burn in their memories. In fact, they've even posted a Web site all about it at www.hotproposal.com.

Here's Todd's story as told to writer Dawn Prince . . .

In 1996, they met when Malissa gave Todd a hair cut at her salon. It only took him the next six years to "muster up the courage to ask her out" as they never seemed to be at same point in their lives. Cupid missed again when Malissa called to cancel that first date because she'd just started dating someone else. But if Cupid was a lousy shot, then timing is everything, because a year later, in 2003, Todd volunteered to fix Malissa's computer. She made him dinner, and over the next week they talked on the phone for hours; they've been together ever since.

One of the things that drew them together is that they're both self-made people with drive and ambition. "Todd is very focused and driven . . . he's got it together," Malissa says, underlining his success. By the time Todd was 20, he was self-employed and making a good deal of money. Today, Todd is CEO and founder of an Internet wholesale company in Grants Pass.

Along with that admiration and appreciation for hard work when they were just friends, over the years they developed a mutual appreciation for each other.

"I felt attracted to Todd for years. While I was cutting his hair, we talked about our travels, our lives," Malissa says. "I did get to know a lot about Todd with our light-hearted discussions. I saw his sense of humor and his level of commitment in his relationships. I had some growing to do in my life, and the timing wasn't what it needed to be."

"I've always been interested in Malissa, but the timing was never right. I value relationships that tenure," he chimes in upon reflection. "I think relationships get richer over time because they season . . . they marinate and take on new flavor. That's what ours did. I like that."

"I really wanted the proposal to be a special event for Malissa because she is just wonderful," Todd says. "I wanted Malissa to have a story to tell—a memorable proposal. It's a gift for the woman I love."

In Grants Pass, Oregon, the Fourth of July was a perfect night for a proposal. It was dusk, and the light was "just so," with the sun going down and night taking over.

Malissa Kusiek and 75 family and friends were gathered for the annual Fourth of July family party, which was to have a few surprises and culminate in fireworks. The crowd thought stuntman and friend Eric Barkey, who's done hundreds of human-torch fire jumps, was to perform a fitting stunt for this occasion. Knowing all safety precautions would be taken to protect him and everyone present, Todd told about a dozen people of his plan, including Malissa's 16-year-old-son Calvin and her sister Mari.

At one point Malissa looked over, and she couldn't understand why her sister was so emotional and even tearing as stunt man "Eric" was getting ready to be set ablaze and jump. It all became clear seconds later.

Hooded and bundled in layers of his water-soaked fire suit and a cape dipped in gasoline, Todd Grannis climbed onto the platform instead of Eric Barkey. Barely able to see out of the hood, Todd found his vision narrowed.

> Hooded and bundled in layers of his water-soaked fire suit and a cape dipped in gasoline, Todd Grannis climbed onto the platform instead of Eric Barkey. Barely able to see out of the hood, Todd found his vision narrowed.

A long aluminum pole fashioned as a torch was lit and put to the cape. Within seconds, he was a fiery, orange ball clearly defined as a man with flames engulfing and shooting off his body.

With Eric and the experienced safety crew standing by, Todd felt surprisingly calm. Without waiting the 20 seconds as Eric suggested, he saw a faint light come around his face, felt a hint of warmth, and decided it was time to jump. Just as they'd rehearsed, arms out, then body folded over in a U-shape with his fists to his toes—only this time with an orange glow—Todd sailed into the air. Flames flowed backward as he dived into the pool.

The scene was spectacular against the night sky, and the screaming crowd stood dazzled. With the flawless stunt now over, Todd tore away the hood.

"When I saw him come out of the pool, my heart was pounding," recalls 36-year-old Malissa, still sounding flushed as she retells the story. "I ran over to him and then to Eric. I was shocked and amazed and laughing all at the same time. All the emotions were going."

The look on Malissa's face was priceless. Everybody was laughing and screaming and having a blast. Before getting down on one knee, Todd said, "Malissa, you make me hot. I want to get the point across that I'm on fire for you."

"I kept laughing, thinking he was so funny. Why was he on his knees?" says Malissa. It wasn't until she saw the ring, she realized, "Oh, my gosh, he's proposing!"

Todd looked up at her and said, "Will you marry me, Malissa?"

Todd then slipped a 2.25-carat diamond ring on Malissa's finger. Thrilled and crying, Malissa blurted, "Yes!"

Wearing a summery blue top and a short white skirt, Malissa was the girl next door, with her natural, pretty features, tousled strawberry-blond hair and radiant smile—a modern version of the fairy princess who had just been asked for her hand by the handsome prince who wanted to honor their love, fire being symbolic of his passion and of the lengths he would go for her.

"I felt like Cinderella," gushes Malissa. "I'd worked hard that morning, and then he put this amazing two-carat ring on my finger. I wasn't expecting it—not that day."

Malissa had known that they would be getting engaged within the next two years, and she says that they talked about marriage half-seriously, although Todd says that after a year into the relationship she gracefully dropped a few hints to which he playfully replied, "Sometime in the next 50 years (wink-wink)."

"I've been very fortunate and dated some truly good ones, but Malissa is the right one," says Todd.

Todd is known for not doing anything in a small way; he likes to have fun, and there seem to be similarities with one of his personal heroes, Richard Branson. Branson is the adventurous, risk-taking hero who has started his own business on ingenuity, traveled to over 30 countries, sky dived, shark dived, rappelled, and bungee jumped off North America's highest platform.

It is this sense of fun and adventure that drew Todd to the idea behind his unusual proposal. Todd had this idea in the back of his mind since the time Eric showed him a picture of himself as he did "the human torch" stunt and said to Todd, "You can do that . . ." as in, "Have an open mind, my friend, embrace your fears, and I'll show you how to do this."

Once the proposal happened, the news quickly spread around the world. Television networks and hundreds of Web sites and newspapers from India to Iraq picked up the story. What Todd thought would be an entertaining story for Malissa to tell has turned into a media rush, with comments from across the country and radio interviews from New York to New Zealand. But tear away the hype of the media, and what you have is a couple who really may be living their own fairytale.

If love enables us to be bigger than we are, then given their approach to love and life, it's easy to see why Todd and Malissa fit so well together. Beautiful, personable, and successful, with genuine love and respect for each other, they seem to be a modern version of the fairytale. And while the proposal has become water cooler talk as the world weighs in on the craziness or the romance of it, they are keeping things in perspective and having fun, as they know all the attention is fleeting.

The two married August 5, 2006, with a simple, elegant ceremony and reception next to the ocean on the island of Kauai, Hawaii, at a botanical garden called Na Aina Kai.

After such a "hot" proposal story, Todd and Malissa are one couple that is glad the flame went out that night (when he plunged into a pool of water), and even more glad that the real spark of love lasts forever.

————

TAKE LOVE TO NEW HEIGHTS

A mountaintop wedding proposal in Canada took this bride's breath away

Beren Tomkies was an assistant director on the movie *Paycheck* as it was being filmed in Vancouver, British Columbia, last May, when her boyfriend Mike decided it was time to take their love to new heights. Here's Beren's story . . .

We now live in Nova Scotia, but at the time Mike and I were both living in Vancouver, where Mike was working as a member of the Royal Canadian Mounted Police. I was working on a film, and we had long hours every day, and finally I had one day off. It was a Sunday, and I was really, really tired, but Mike came to me and said, "You now, it's such a nice day, and I have planned something fun for us today, OK? But first I have to go out and get some food for a picnic."

It was May, and though it was clear and sunny and beautiful, Mike said to pack something warm and bring some towels to sit on for our picnic. So I got things together, and soon he returned with our food, and we started driving north. It was supposed to be a surprise, but I realized we were driving toward the Vancouver airport. I had no idea what we were doing or who we were going with or what Mike was up to, but I figured it was a boat ride, since the Vancouver airport has a lot of docks there nearby on the bay.

Mike said, "I just have to go into a hangar and talk to a friend for a minute." So we pulled into an area with private hangars, got out, walked past a couple of helicopters, and went into the second hangar where a friend of Mike's, a helicopter pilot named Peter, was there with his girlfriend.

Peter said, "Are you guys ready?"

And I said, "Ready? What do you mean?" We all walked out the door where a helicopter was waiting, and Mike said, "Yeah, we're going for a little ride!"

I was so excited—it isn't every day you get to go on a helicopter ride. So we all climbed in and Peter gave us a tour above the city of Vancouver. We flew over the mountain range called the Lions, which you see against the skyline of Vancouver. It was so lovely. Then Peter dropped Mike and me off on one of the little mountain peaks and said, "We'll be back to get you in a couple of hours." He and his girlfriend took off in the helicopter.

"We're going to have a nice little picnic up here," Mike said. It was a cool, crisp, beautiful sunny day on that mountaintop mesa.

Mike thought of everything. We ate pâtés and little crackers and drank sparkling wine that he brought. We were talking and having a great time.

But then, Mike looked at me, and I immediately had this amazing feeling. I knew something was up.

As I was reaching for another cracker, Mike grabbed my hand. He had taken off his big engineering ring and he slipped it on my finger. He said, "Will you marry me?" and I said, "Yes!" He said, "This ring is only temporary until I can get you one."

> "It was the perfect moment, and the perfect proposal. I was completely and utterly shocked! I'd had no idea. Of course I said 'yes.'"

It was the perfect moment, and the perfect proposal. I was completely and utterly shocked! I'd had no idea. Of course I said "yes." There we were, helicoptered to the peak of the mountain for a picnic. It was rocky where we were, but he still got down on his knee. It was really, really sweet. I'll never forget this mountaintop experience with the guy I love.

"We're getting married in Barbados on May 25–four years later," says Beren.

Some things are worth waiting for, and we hope this couple's mountaintop experience is a rocky mountain high that never ends.

———

IT'S UP TO YOU, NEW YORK, NEW YORK!

"If I can make it there, I'll make it anywhere," thought one San Diego man, so he and his love took a bite out of the Big Apple, where he had a surprise waiting in Times Square

Perhaps no city in America is as bustling with excitement as New York City, so what better place for a mind-blowing proposal than at the apex of this bright lights, big city destination– Times Square. Here's a story that diamond expert Fred Cuellar told us about. The story was submitted by groom-to-be Jeran Fraser, a San Diego real estate investor who now lives in Incline Village, Nevada, and is told by his bride-to-be, Lauren Kishpaugh . . .

My fiancé has always been the romantic type, but what he did for my proposal was absolutely incredible.

On the morning of my birthday he woke me up at 5 a.m. and told me to pack my bags with summer clothes. At 7 a.m. we were on our way to New York from San Diego.

As we arrived in New York, I noticed he had everything planned, which included roses and chocolate on my pillow at the hotel. I wasn't quite sure what to expect that day, but a wedding proposal was not in the plans . . . or was it?

We spent the next few days experiencing the beauty of New York, which was a first for both of us. During the week, Jeran seemed to have an infatuation with Times Square. Wednesday and Thursday were extremely hot, and he had pointed out to me that a few of the billboards had been turned off due to the heat wave, which was an extreme rarity in Times Square.

That Friday evening, when the air was finally beginning to cool, he told me to dress up because we were going to have a nice dinner. We jumped in a cab, and stopped about two blocks from Times Square. I still had no idea of what was about to happen.

> "That Friday evening, when the air was finally beginning to cool, he told me to dress up because we were going to have a nice dinner. We jumped in a cab, and stopped about two blocks from Times Square. I still had no idea of what was about to happen."

We walked around for about ten minutes, and then he pointed up to the Reuters' billboard at Times Square. On the giant billboard was a picture of our first trip together and our first kiss on the beach. As I looked further I saw a poem scrolling on the bottom of the photo that read:

"This day is as special as each day in our life, on this night I ask you WILL YOU BE MY WIFE?"

As the message scrolled, a few other photos followed the initial photo.

I turned around to look at him, and he was down on his knee in the middle of Times Square with a ring and poem in his hand.

At the same time, I noticed a photographer taking pictures of the whole event. I fell into a state of shock and literally was speechless for 30 seconds, after which time I gathered myself and answered his proposal with a, "Yes!"

The proposal was followed by a wonderful dinner and a Broadway show that was fitting for the occasion, *The Wedding Singer.*

The couple's marriage is planned for August, a year to the day since the spectacular engagement!

According to a *San Diego Union Tribune* story about the event, Fraser was starting to sweat a bit when the heat wave nearly ruined the proposal by causing the huge "spectaculars," or electronic billboards, to shut down for several days. It had taken quite a bit of work to get his proposal and photos up on the sign.

"After contacting several outdoor advertising companies without success, Fraser learned about Nationwide's Life Comes At You Fast ad campaign. The insurance company had leased an electronic billboard in Times Square and was posting photos and text messages submitted to its Web site from the public. So Fraser e-mailed his story.

"A few days later he learned that his photos would be shown about 5 p.m., July 31 through Aug. 4. It was perfect timing—until, that is, he lured Kishpaugh to Times Square on Aug. 2 and the board was dark because of energy conservation during the heat wave. On Aug. 3, the board still was dark. On Aug. 4, the final night, he learned it was working again," writes Diane Bell of SignOnSanDiego.com by the *Union Tribune*.

HOW TO PLAN A "SPECTACULAR" PROPOSAL AT TIMES SQUARE

The huge electronic signs that light up Times Square 24/7 are called "spectaculars" by the billboard industry, and we can certainly understand why. These impressive signs can stand stories tall and seem to be the center of one of the hottest cities on the planet. Seeing her name in lights on Broadway and 45th would make almost any woman swoon. But surprisingly, a Times Square proposal is far less expensive than you might guess.

To have a photo of you holding the ring (or just a photo of the two of you) and words such as, "Will you marry me, Carrie?" up on a spectacular at Times Square, all you have to do is walk into the Toys "R" Us Times Square store in New York, pay a modest $29.99, and they'll take your photo, take down the information you want on the sign, ask you what time you want it to be on the 40-x-50-foot Times Square sign (at 44th and Broadway), and arrange to have someone there to photograph the moment you propose to her. The package, costing under $30, includes the air time on the board and a 5x7 photograph of you and your love taken live at the moment of the proposal. You can walk into the store and do this on the spot and see your proposal up on the sign five minutes later! Or you can arrange for it to be shown that night as you're walking by at a carefully pre-arranged time.

For more information, call Toys "R" Us Times Square at (646) 366-8863, 1293 Broadway, New York, NY 10001-2910.

SWEETS FOR THE SWEET
AT TIMES SQUARE

How sweet it is that the Hershey's Times Square store not only sells fabulous chocolates, it will give your proposal its 15 minutes of fame, quite literally. Hershey's charges only $4.95 to have your proposal run for 15 minutes on their big spectacular in Times Square at 49th and Broadway. The only downside is that they don't put up photos—only text. Still, nothing could be sweeter than sharing a Hershey's kiss while asking her to be yours forever on a huge Hershey's spectacular electronic billboard on Times Square.

For more information call Hershey's Times Square at (212) 581-9100, 1593 Broadway, New York, NY 10019-7406.

BIG EASY PROPOSAL

"Throw Me Somethin', Mister!"

Megan Bronson of New Orleans, Louisiana, has always loved surprises. Her boyfriend Andy knew that never before had New Orleans or Megan needed a better Mardi Gras and a bigger surprise than they did in February, 2007, just eighteen months after Hurricane Katrina hit the southern Gulf Coast states, flooding more than 80 percent of the city of New Orleans. Here is Megan's story of the best Mardi Gras surprise ever . . .

"As the float approached, I ran off to meet it, and the crowd behind me released a collective 'Oh, No!'"

We can never surprise each other. We love surprises—big ones, little ones—but inevitably one of us stumbles upon clues and figures them out, much to the disappointment of the other.

Well, this time Andy finally got me, and in a huge way.

Andy invited both sets of our parents to come visit for what I thought was a Mardi Gras/wedding anniversary weekend. We arranged to have a lovely dinner at Emeril's restaurant in New Orleans for Friday night, to go on the Katrina "devastation tour" Saturday, and go watch a Mardi Gras King Arthur parade on Sunday.

Sunday rolled around, and we were all excited about the parade–or so I thought.

The week prior to the visit, Andy had been mentioning more and more people he wanted to invite to the parade on Sunday. I figured it was because several of our friends would be riding on floats in the parade. Why wouldn't we want all of our buddies there to catch as much stuff–as many Mardi Gras "throws"–from our friends as possible? That's what the parades are all about.

When we got there, I saw a good dozen or so of our friends already in position. More and more people we knew kept arriving. There must have been 30 or more of our extended New Orleans family. It was such a blessing, because we had a chance to introduce them to our respective parents.

I continued in my happy world of parade watching and couldn't wait for Jerry's float to arrive. I was positive I was going to catch a ton of stuff! Float 11 rolled by, and a general murmur went through the crowd.

"It's the next one. It's coming up. Here it comes." I could hear all these things as Andy took me by the shoulders and guided me to the front. No one impeded us, and I thought how lovely my friends are; they are so generous with sharing the front row.

As the float approached, I ran off to meet it, and the crowd behind me released a collective "Oh, No!" I raced up to the float, and our friend Michael who was beside Jerry on the float tossed me a giant Grover stuffed animal and a couple unopened packages of large beads. Our friends, Celia and Jenny, grabbed the back of my shirt to tug me back to Andy's side.

Of course I was annoyed. Why would they keep me from getting as much "stuff" as possible from a friend on a float? This is terrible New Orleans Mardi Gras parade etiquette, and they were going to hear it from me just as soon as the float passed.

Well, they saved the day. Jenny tapped my shoulder and in a very serene voice said, "Look what Andy just caught."

Since I was too preoccupied with trying to get stuff from the float, I had missed seeing Jerry throwing Andy a ring box, as well as Andy's catching it and quickly exchanging it with one our friend David was carrying. Jerry's box was kept empty just in case it accidentally got tossed to the wrong person or accidentally was dropped, and David had the real ring ready.

By the time I turned to Andy, he was down on one knee with the open ring box and a beautiful aquamarine ring—he knows I'm very, very opposed to diamonds. Aquamarines, I love, however. That's my birthstone, and in Hebrew, Roman, or Arabic cultures, I'm told, it's also the birthstone for October, which is Andy's birth month.

At any rate, there he was on bended knee with this beautiful engagement ring. I couldn't believe it was really happening. Everything I had been holding immediately dropped from my arms as I heard him say, "Will you marry me?"

I nodded and squeaked out a, "Yes, yes! Of course!"

7

THE ROMANTIC

Romantic moments can come in big or small packages. Romance can be a walk in the rain through a meadow, a carriage ride in Central Park, a quiet dinner for two at your favorite restaurant, a bottle of champagne and a bubble bath, rose petals at her feet, or just Eskimo kisses on a winter day. If the one you love goes for the romantic gesture, big or small, the marriage proposal should be an event when you pull out all the stops to make her heart stop and her knees go weak. You've got to make her swoon.

SEE VENICE AND DIE

(Or, rather, swoon)

This story comes from Jeff Catalina and his bride, Erin. This story could easily have fit in the "Extremist" chapter on proposal stories, but it was so romantic we swooned while typing it, so here goes . . .

Erin tells the story . . .

"So I'm thinking Spanish food for dinner on Saturday," said Jeff. It sounded good to me,

> "My senses were so overloaded as I took in the lively and mysterious atmosphere that I was rendered speechless."

and for the rest of the week I looked forward to the mystery restaurant where Jeff would treat me to a belated birthday and Valentine's Day dinner. When Saturday came around my morning routine was just that . . . routine. Cereal for breakfast, a three-mile run, and then it was off to Jeff's. When I arrived there was a shoebox-sized gift labeled #1 waiting for me. I knew it was a disguise. What I never would have guessed was that the box disguised two tickets to Madrid! As I stared at them, all I could manage to say was, "When?!?"

The answer? "We're leaving at 4:50 this afternoon, so go home and pack a bag."

"What about work?" I asked. Jeff had already e-mailed my boss, and my boss gladly granted my vacation.

"What should I wear?"

"Fall temperature clothes, but bring a nice coat."

I packed feverishly, called my family, and soon we were flying into the wild blue yonder.

Just before departure, Jeff said, "I'm sorry, but Madrid's not exactly where we're going, so we have to catch another short flight after this one." Seven hours later, we found ourselves in Madrid's customs line, and then, out of the backpack came #2 and the camera.

"So I changed my mind . . . I'm thinking Italian for dinner tonight," said Jeff. Gift #2 was a map of Venice! Jeff mumbled assurance that there were no more surprises, except some information I'd hear on the plane. We were staying on the Grand Canal at *Palazzo Sant'angelo,* a palace converted into a small hotel, with its own gondola port. Furthermore, we would be in *Venezia* for the last three days of *Carnivale,* the traditional masquerade festival preceding the Lenten season. We would go on a private gondola tour, to the glassmaking island of Murano, and to an orchestra concert.

After checking into the hotel and stashing our luggage, Jeff and I wandered to Piazza San Marco to join the festivities. I had never seen anything like it; masses of people crowding narrow cobblestone streets, face painters, street musicians, and costumes with more colors than I could count. My senses were so overloaded as I took in the lively and mysterious atmosphere that I was rendered speechless. Jeff asked a passerby to take a photo of us by the Grand Canal. After, he turned to me, professed his love, and with shaking hand unveiled a . . . wallet.

Oops, missed.

With no further delay, Jeff dropped down on one knee, presented me with a beautiful ring, and asked me to marry him.

I stood there crying and looking at the ring until Jeff finally said, "So are you going to put it on?"

I choked out a, "Yes!" and, thus, a new adventure began.

——

WHEN YOU GET CAUGHT BETWEEN THE MOON AND NEW YORK CITY THE BEST THAT YOU CAN DO IS FALL IN LOVE

—Christopher Cross, *Love Theme* from *Arthur*

Harrison Grant Wise, vice president of Rubenstein Public Relations, Inc., of New York, disregarded our advice and did things his own way, even ignoring his bride-to-be's desires about the kind of ring she thought she wanted. He must have known her better than she knew herself, for she wasn't disappointed at all when he surprised her with an over-the-top proposal, over the top of skyscrapers and the Statue of Liberty.

Harrison recalls how his romantic proposal turned out just right for him and Tara, his bride-to-be. He thought it was romantic to take his love to new heights—and he was right.

"So when I blindfolded Tara near the Chelsea Piers, she was thinking, 'This jerk bought a boat!' But that wasn't it at all."

Here's Harrison's story . . .

After spending a Thanksgiving in Puerto Rico one year after we started dating, my (now) fiancée, Tara Padua, was expecting that I would propose. But since that took some of the fun and mystique out of it, I decided to do it in a way that was sure to surprise her.

On New Year's Eve, my mother offered to take Tara for a manicure, pedicure, and hairstyle as a late Christmas present. Unbeknownst to Laura, my mom was laying down the groundwork for what was to be an evening to remember.

Afterward, Tara and I met up with some friends at Villa Paradiso, an old-school Italian restaurant in Bensonhurst, Brooklyn, for a relaxed dinner. At around 10:30 p.m., a white stretch-limo pulled up to the curb. I told Tara that they didn't have any more taxis, so they sent us a limo to take us into Manhattan, where we had planned to meet some friends. Once we arrived in the city, I said, "There's something I want to show you." All week I had been ogling boats at the New York International Boat Show at The Javits Center and proclaiming my desire to own one of those boats. So when I blindfolded Tara near the Chelsea Piers, she was thinking, "This jerk bought a boat!" But that wasn't it at all.

The limo pulled into a heliport on the West Side Highway, and within minutes Tara and I found ourselves circling around the Statue of Liberty in a private helicopter (a luxury Sikorsky) that I'd chartered just for the occasion. I had the finest rosé champagne on ice and chocolate-covered strawberries waiting for us.

As we flew over Manhattan, I got down on bended knee and presented Tara with a 1.5-carat, brilliant-cut, platinum-pavé-set diamond from Riverfront Jewelers in Battery Park City. I told Tara that this city and this world are ours to share and experience together, and with the bird's-eye view we had, those words had the impact I was looking for.

I assured Tara that the ring wasn't for her (she had at one point insisted she didn't want any "blood diamonds"). "It's for your girl-friends," I told her.

After landing about 45 minutes later, we took the limo to all of our friends' houses to share the magic of our evening.

That's our story; Tara still gets teary-eyed whenever I tell it.

———

WATCH OUT! THAT FIRST STEP/THAT FIRST KISS IS A DOOSIE!

A Chicago couple returns to the scene of their first kiss

You don't have to rent a helicopter or spend a lot of money to create a memorable, romantic moment. This wise Chicago guy knew that even small things can mean a lot if done with love. Here is a story from a guy named Mike who remembered a wish his girlfriend had—she always hoped that one day they'd re-enact their first kiss at the same spot where it had happened years ago.

It was January 31, 2001, and it was a typical Chicago New Year's Eve: ice cold. Yet the ice I was carrying (the diamond ring, of course) could have burned a hole in my pocket. I've been told most guys are nervous before they pop the big question, but I wasn't at all. I knew in my heart Elizabeth was "the one." Instead, the feeling I had was that of anticipation, for I had the perfect plan to surprise my girlfriend and make it a memorable experience for both of us.

Before the clock hits midnight on this night we have to rewind two years earlier to the end

"I have to say, it was a great kiss. We were both a little buzzed from the beer, so we held it for a good 15 to 20 seconds. As our lips unlocked, I just knew, and when she looked into my eyes I knew she knew, too."

of our very first date. We were both Broadcast Journalism majors at Columbia College. Somehow, after years at the same school, we had never been in the same class until then, our senior year. After two hours of great conversation over a couple pints of Guinness at a local pub downtown, I walked Elizabeth to her subway stop at the corner of Washington and Dearborn. It was there at the top of the steps leading down to the subway that sparks flared as we shared our first kiss.

I have to say, it was a great kiss. We were both a little buzzed from the beer, so we held it for a good 15 to 20 seconds. As our lips unlocked, I just knew, and when she looked into my eyes I knew she knew, too.

While dating, we would often pass by the same subway stop. Like clockwork, Elizabeth would always turn to me, smile, bat her eyelashes and say, "Aw, look, baby; that's where we had our first kiss. Let's stop and re-enact it."

I would roll my eyes (she never saw that) and reply, "Oh, one day, honey."

She'd pout for a minute and then get over it.

This would happen every few months or so. Soon she was actually getting mad at me for not stopping for the "re-enact kiss." By this time, I was refusing not because I wasn't being romantic or sentimental; rather, I had wised up. We were getting serious about our relationship. What better place to ask her to marry me? And since she bugged me all the time about it anyway, I knew she would never suspect a thing!

Fast-forward now to the night of nights. I picked up Elizabeth and we headed toward the bar where all our friends were waiting in anticipation. They all knew I was going to propose to Elizabeth that night, but as far as I could tell she still didn't suspect it at all. While in the car, I spun my well-thought-out white lie. I explained I had to pick something up at a downtown store for my mom. I pretended the store was near the subway stop. But when I stopped to park a block from the subway stop, she caught me in the lie . . . geographically speaking. You see, Elizabeth can get around downtown blindfolded.

"Mike, what are you doing? The store you said we need to go to is six blocks away!"

Luckily I could think on my feet, so I simply replied, "Oh, well, it's a nice night, let's just walk," to which she snapped back, "Are you kidding? It's like two degrees out! Why don't you just pull up to the store and jump out?"

Now, at this point I would usually fight back. Instead I just laughed. This enraged her even more, and for a minute, Elizabeth refused to get out of the car. Again, I just laughed and insisted we walk.

If her mind hadn't been so clouded by anger, she might have figured out what was going on. Turns out, I was nervous after all, because when I get nervous, I laugh. Elizabeth knows this. The situation made the moment that much sweeter. In about three minutes I knew she was going to be begging for my forgiveness through tears of joy . . . unless of course she said, "No!"

We looked like Eskimos as we crossed Dearborn Street. Like a scared turtle, Elizabeth had her head so far tucked down in her jacket she didn't even notice where we were. I had to grab her by the wrist to stop her.

Her head quickly popped out and she said with a big smile on her face, "Aw, baby. You finally remembered!"

I kissed her once. "That was for the past," I said softly.

I kissed her a second time. "That was for the present," I said even more softly. She now looked perplexed.

I kissed her a third time, dropped to one knee, dug out the ring from my pocket in perfect form and said without a stumble, "And this is for the future. Elizabeth, will you marry me?"

The combination of the shock and cold stunned her.

I had pulled it off!

Then the tears began, along with an ear-to-ear smile.

"Oh my God, baby! Oh my God!" she exclaimed.

I took that as a yes.

Then, as an afterthought, "I was such a jerk to you! I feel like such a fool. You had me so confused. Do you forgive me?" she asked.

I replied using my best suave, sarcastic tone, "Well, if you say yes, I will!"

"Oops!" she gasped. "Of *course* I will marry you!"

A select few Chicagoans braving the cold and walking by clapped and congratulated us.

I picked Elizabeth up and twirled her around a couple times, and we kissed again.

I'd never felt warmer in my life.

———

IT'S THE LITTLE THINGS THAT COUNT

Small romantic touches can make all the difference...
but a jar of chocolate sauce?

As the owners of Rancho de San Juan in New Mexico, one of the most luxurious country inns and resorts in the United States, Relais and Châteaux see romantic proposals all the time. The resort includes a fabulous Sandstone Shrine built into the side of a natural rock outcropping and has huge glass windows overlooking the desert mountain landscape and the resort property. The Sandstone Shrine, or "Windows in the Earth," as it is sometimes called, is often the site of small, intimate weddings. The Shrine is a very easy 10- to 15-minute hike from the restaurant, suites, and private casitas. It is also a good spot for a private, almost sacred proposal. Owner and executive chef John H. Johnson, III, and owner and director David Heath share with us five of the most romantic ways guys have proposed to their sweethearts at Rancho de San Juan.

TOP FIVE ROMANTIC WAYS TO PROPOSE

1. **Bubbly and bling.** At the restaurant, several guests have requested that the engagement ring be delivered to the table in a glass of champagne, which we always serve on a silver tray.

2. **Delicious diamond.** Others have requested that the ring be put on top of the lady's dessert when it is served, propped on top of the whipped cream or placed on a cookie to the side. In a more modern approach, we actually had a lady who proposed to her boyfriend that way.

3. **Chocolate and charm.** Of course, the traditional "rose petals on the bed" with a bottle of champagne and special chocolates is another favorite proposal tactic. One couple actually requested a jar of chocolate sauce to be placed by the bed ... Now that's imagination! Strangely enough, there was no chocolate on the bedding the next day.

4. **Tub for two.** One gentleman had us set the bucket with champagne and glasses by the whirlpool tub in their room, along with the ring box and candles, while they were having dinner in the restaurant. They took their dessert back to the room with them.

5. **Going public.** People love getting engaged in the dining room at the restaurant. I guess it's romantic to propose at the table in front of the fireplace. A lot of people seem to like public proposals—it adds to the excitement when others share their joy.

8

CELEBRITY PROPOSALS

S ome guys have all the luck; they get the girl and ride off into the sunset, as well as being a star on the silver screen. Whether you're a supermodel, a superstar, or you're a TV reporter for a local station, all eyes are on you when you get engaged. The following stories feature some famous people whose public proposals left their fans speechless.

THE "TOMKAT" PARIS PROPOSAL

He took her to the City of Lights and proposed at the Eiffel Tower

In mid-June, Paris is arguably one of the most romantic places in the world. It was in that month that Tom Cruise took his new love, young Katie Holmes, to dine at the Eiffel Tower. According to reports, Tom had never been there before, but he had a hunch this romantic setting would be the perfect place to pop the question. The next day, having not slept at all, the happy couple attended a press conference with Dakota Fanning to talk about the *War of the Worlds*, a film Cruise and Fanning were promoting, and *Batman Begins*, which Katie was promoting. However, the proposal of the night before was all anyone could talk about. Holmes was quiet except to gush, "I'm so happy."

One reporter asked Cruise, "Was that the most fun in Paris that you've ever had?"

Cruise smiled and replied, "Yes. Without question, the most special time in Europe ever."

He went on to explain, "The [movie] premier we wanted here in France, because it's beautiful and it's romantic. And yes, I proposed to Kate last night."

Katie wore the ring to prove it. The two had only dated for about two months, but everyone knew about their courtship—especially after Tom went a little crazy on *Oprah* by jumping on the couch and shouting declarations of love for Katie on the air.

Their courtship first began in Rome that April, but Tom chose Paris for the proposal setting because it is such a romantic city, explaining, "I don't want to disappoint her." By the look of the huge rock on her finger and the big smile on Katie's face, Tom obviously didn't have to worry about that.

The couple exchanged Scientology wedding vows in a ceremony at Odescalchi Castle in Italy on November 18, 2006, after Katie had already given birth to a baby daughter, Suri. According to Associated Press reports, an exchange of vows with a Scientology rite is not legally recognized in Italy, and would have to be preceded or followed by a civil union. But the couple had thought ahead and had arranged a civil service in California several weeks prior to the Italian wedding ceremony, making the marriage legal and the Paris proposal all worthwhile.

———

THE ROYAL "WE"

How the Queen of England Got Her Prince

Prince Philip proposed to Queen Elizabeth II in 1946 while the two were walking on the grounds of Balmoral, the royal family's castle in Scotland, on a sunny day.

"It was wonderful, magical," Elizabeth reportedly said later. "I just threw my arms round his neck and kissed him as he held me to him, my feet off the ground."

The couple kept their news quiet, knowing Elizabeth's father would disapprove due to her young age. She was twenty at the time; Philip was twenty-five. But the story soon leaked to the press. Elizabeth's father, King George VI, was angry to learn that Philip and Elizabeth hadn't asked for his permission prior to the engagement, and it was not until the next year that he agreed to let them marry. They were finally wed in November, 1947.

Elizabeth II and Prince Philip are still married. In 1997, they celebrated their 50th anniversary.

PRINCE CHARMING HE'S NOT

"Whatever Love Means"

Prince Charles' proposal to Lady Diana Spencer wasn't the fairy-tale romance you might expect from a prince. It was reported at the time by the royal family that Charles had proposed at a dinner at Buckingham Palace while the couple sipped champagne. But that's not how Diana remembered it. According to her, it really happened just as she told it to Andrew Morton for his 1992 biography *Diana*. Diana claims that Prince Charles proposed to her in the nursery of Windsor Castle.

"He said, 'Will you marry me?' and I laughed. I remember thinking, 'This is a joke,' and I said, 'Yeah, OK,' and laughed. He was deadly serious," said Diana.

"He said, 'You do realize that one day you will

> "He said, 'Will you marry me?' and I laughed. I remember thinking, 'This is a joke,' and I said, 'Yeah, OK,' and laughed. He was deadly serious," said Diana.

be Queen?' And a voice said to me inside, 'You won't be Queen, but you'll have a tough role.'

So I said, 'Yes.' I said, 'I love you so much. I love you so much.'

He said, 'Whatever love means.'"

Years later, after Diana the Princess of Wales had been killed in an automobile crash in Paris, Prince Charles proposed to long-time mistress Camilla Parker-Bowles. According to reports, he did it on bended knee and presented her with a big diamond ring. When they married, he vowed to love her.

Whatever that means.

―――

RIVER WALK REPORTER ROMANCE

San Antonio Television News Reporter Floated into Engagement on a River Walk Boat

Nancy Salazar is a popular news reporter and anchor of the successful ABC affiliate show *Good Morning San Antonio*, and has a loyal following of viewers in the nation's seventh largest city. Salazar also had a big following on the day she got engaged. Lots of onlookers were nearby as her boyfriend proposed to her on the romantic San Antonio River Walk, a popular tourist area that is also a favorite of locals, especially lovers who enjoy its magical ambience. Here's the story that now husband and wife Gabriel and Nancy Salazar tell . . .

> "I was growing impatient. I was mad, in fact. All I kept thinking was that I needed to get back home and go to bed."

We had dated for about six years, and I knew we would be married eventually. But my husband, who is always good at keeping the romance alive, came up with the perfect plan that he somehow kept secret from me for months. I'm a news reporter, so I pride myself in uncovering the truth and being keenly observant. But I totally missed this one!

It was Sunday, and Gabriel said we needed to meet some of his colleagues in downtown San Antonio for a business dinner. I didn't want to go. I have to wake up every morning at 3:30 a.m. to anchor *Good Morning San Antonio*, so I go to bed early. But Gabriel insisted that all the other guys would have their wives with them and he needed me there. I wasn't happy, but I agreed to sacrifice my sleep to go with him.

We arrived downtown and he immediately got on the cell phone to locate his "colleagues." We went to the restaurant area of the San Antonio River Walk and found one of his friends, Jaime, who told us that everyone was running late and that our reservations had been lost. He and Gabriel both got on their cell phones (supposedly) to get the reservations right and get "everyone" organized. I was growing impatient. I was mad, in fact. All I kept thinking was that I needed to get back home and go to bed.

Finally, Gabriel and Jaime said it was time to go to the restaurant. For a second I thought, "Well, where the heck is everyone else?" But I figured "Whatever. Let's just get to the restaurant."

As Gabriel led me along the River Walk, I noticed a river barge in the water that had a dinner table on it, decorated with roses, rose petals, and candles. On the barge, I saw one of my friends named Rudy, who's a professional saxophonist. I said to Gabriel, "Look! There's Rudy! Wow, I wonder what he's doing here."

I thought we were going to keep on walking, but Gabriel suggested we stop to say hello to Rudy.

I said, "Gabriel, Rudy's on a gig. This is somebody's special day. This is somebody's barge." There was no way I was going to climb onto some stranger's boat and interrupt Rudy in the middle of a job.

Still, Gabriel led me on and I waved hello. Rudy just smiled. Feeling even more awkward, I turned to Gabriel, who was suddenly looking nervous.

In a quivering voice he said, "My baby, this is *your* boat."

At that moment, my heart skipped a beat, my eyes filled with tears, and a huge lump rose in my throat.

Finally, I realized that my Gabriel was about to propose to me.

Rudy started to play our song, *Always and Forever,* and the boat began cruising along the San Antonio River.

Gabriel had me sit at a table that was set for two. He got down on both knees and uttered some incoherent words, professing his love for me. But don't ask me what he said, because all I cared about was getting that ring on my finger. I'm not even sure if he officially asked me the magical question before I yelled an enthusiastic, "Yes!"

The newly lit Christmas lights sparkled along the River Walk as we sailed. It was a truly amazing evening.

9

AT THE GAME

While the first proposal story here is about a celebrity, we thought we'd save it for this chapter because it included a big, public sports-event proposal. If the girl likes her sports, this may be the way to go. It's hard to say no with thousands of cheering fans.

ALL-STAR PROPOSAL

The View Talk Show Co-Host Star Jones

On February, 15, 2004, Al Reynolds, boyfriend of daytime television celebrity Star Jones, scored some very big points with his sweetheart at a big NBA game. At the beginning of the fourth quarter, Reynolds proposed in a very big, very public way at the NBA All-Star game in Los Angeles. Down on one knee, he promised to love her for the rest of her life as he gave her a princess-cut diamond engagement ring.

It's hard to say who was more surprised—Star Jones, or the basketball fans in the stadium. The couples' families weren't surprised, though. Reynolds had already asked his mother for her blessing on February 11, and on February 12, Al surprised Star by bringing her family to New York to ask their permission for her hand in marriage.

According to newspaper reports, the couple enjoyed an engagement party on March 27, 2004, at the Supper Club in New York City.

The two were married in a lavish ceremony later that year in New York City.

———

THANKSGIVING DAY FOOTBALL TOUCHDOWN

The half-time show was great this time

Before millions of viewers, and while delivering half-time commentary during a 1985 Thanksgiving Day football game, Ahmad Rashad asked *The Cosby Show*'s own Phylicia Ayers Allen to marry him. She said, "Yes," of course. No pressure: it was only a nationally televised game with most of America watching.

———

GET YOUR KICKS WITH THE NY KNICKS

Propose at Madison Square Garden

Interested in staging your own message-board proposal at Madison Square Garden during a New York Knicks Game? It is surprisingly inexpensive and easy to set up. Just contact Kathleen Decker at (212) 465-6409, or e-mail her at kathleen.decker@thegarden.com. The cost is $100, and the money goes to the Garden of Dreams Foundation. Your proposal message will run during half-time. One goody bag will be delivered to the recipient's seat during the third quarter of the game. You know you're going to score points with this kind of proposal if she's a Knicks fan!

———

FISHING TALE

He didn't want her to be the "one that got away"

Not every sportsman, however, has to stage a big, public proposal. One of the rules of engagement is to make the moment about the two of you and the things you both enjoy doing together. Dan Armitage is an outdoor enthusiast, hunting and fishing writer, and radio talk-show host in Ohio. His proposal story is about a special fishing trip with the most special woman in his life. It is private and sweet, and his love for her is apparent in every word. Here's his story . . .

> "There she was in tattered pants, smoke in her eyes, having to bathe in an icy lake every evening, eating wall-eye with sand in it, washing it down with lukewarm beer, and I realized how lucky I was."

I was researching a how-to book, and I enjoy a Canadian fly-in fishing vacation, and so I visited a different lodge in Canada each summer. Maria had been to several of these lodges with me while we dated, and we really enjoy the solitude and adventure these fishing vacations would offer us. At the camps, each party or couple was given a boat to use for the week, and most days were spent on the lakes and rivers fishing and exploring. Many of the guests took along a shore lunch kit to allow them to cook and eat their catch without having to return to the lodge or cabin to eat. The kit usually included potatoes; butter or lard; a can of beans; bacon; maybe bread or muffin mix; milk and bread crumbs for making batter; and onions, all in a giant, ancient, oily cast-iron frying pan. Maria and I would usually spend our mornings going around in the boat looking for a nice beach or scenic island on which to build a fire, cook our catch, enjoy lunch, and lie around.

When we would find the right spot and lunch time arrived, we'd have a contest. I'd pull up to shore and let Maria off with matches and the lunch kit, and she'd get busy making a lunch camp. I had to catch enough fish (usually two or three walleye or perch) in the time it took to get a fire built and the lunch area set-up. It's something we'd done dozens of times before on other lakes while staying at other lodges and camps, and we both loved it.

Just before this one trip, however, Maria had been involved in a traffic accident, and I had been called to the hospital—not knowing her condition. During that drive, I realized how much she meant to me and how I didn't want to spend the rest of my life without her. And so I decided then and there to ask her to marry me when the right time came. I was so thankful and relieved when Maria recovered from the crash, having suffered only minor injuries.

The right time came that summer, just after a particularly nice shore lunch, doing something we both loved. There she was in tattered pants, smoke in her eyes, having to bathe in an icy lake every evening, eating walleye with sand in it, washing it down with lukewarm beer, and I realized how lucky I was.

It was spontaneous; I didn't have a ring, but I just dropped to one knee and asked while she was sitting on a rock on the beach looking at the water.

She thought I was kidding, but she said, "Yes."

She asked me later that night if I meant it, and if it "counted," and I said it did.

That's my biggest, best fishing tale!

10

BOTCHED PROPOSALS

Here's the chapter you've been dreading: the true-life stories of guys who got shot down because they didn't know the rules of engagement. The names have been changed to protect the humiliated and broken-hearted, but these stories are true, so read them and weep, live and learn.

RELATIONSHIP OPTIONAL

He had a ring, so what else did he need?

This is a true story from a woman in Louisiana who has turned down proposals twice. As you read about this one, you can understand why . . .

I was sitting in a tavern, the college hangout where we all went in the evenings for wine coolers and pitchers of beer, with my roommate's ex-boyfriend. He's a sweet guy, but I always felt a bit sorry for him because he was rather inept when it came to women. The funny thing is, my roommate was still crazy about this guy, but the relationship never

> "I don't recall exactly what I said, but it was something like, 'But we're not even dating! You can't be serious!' And I reminded him that my best friend happened to be in love with him."

seemed to go anywhere. She dreamed that one day they'd marry, but it never happened, and I secretly wondered if he were gay. Anyway, we were talking casually when he said, 'I have my grandmother's ring in my pocket, and I was wondering if you might marry me.'

I looked at him incredulously, and then I realized he was totally serious.

I don't recall exactly what I said, but it was something like, "But we're not even dating! You can't be serious!" And I reminded him that my best friend happened to be in love with him.

He looked wounded, but just for a moment. Almost as nonchalantly as he asked me, he put the ring back in his pocket and started speculating about other people he could ask. He said he really wanted to get married.

I patted him on the shoulder as I walked off to the restroom, shaking my head.

———

THE WEDDING PUT HIM IN THE MOOD

Three weeks and never been kissed? Don't ask.

Lori, in Texas, tells this story of a sweet, but also ill-conceived and premature, proposal.

Ed and I had been going out very casually for just a few weeks, and the guy was a sweetheart who sent flowers to me all the time at work. I kind of liked him, but the chemistry seemed a little 'off' for me, so I'd limited our dates to lunches in the middle of the day and group things until I could tell if I even liked the guy. So far, I thought he was sweet, but I knew I was 'just not that into him.' I was sure I'd made that clear; I'd never really kissed him the whole three weeks we went out except once, only very politely at that, at the end of a lunch date. But still he seemed crazy about me and didn't hide his feelings. So I started trying to discourage him. I told him he shouldn't send me flowers, and I didn't want to go out to lunch anymore.

One Saturday afternoon, not long after I'd done my best to let him know I just wanted to be friends, we both happened to be attending a wedding of a mutual friend. We were standing outside the entrance of the hotel where the reception was going to take place, and we were making small talk about how we wished the happy couple well.

That's when he did it. He turned to me with tears in his eyes and said, "I think we should get married."

I involuntarily spit out a wild, "What!?"

At first he didn't seem to notice how surprised and appalled I was.

"Will you marry me?" he begged, and he started to get down on one knee.

"No, don't do that! Get up!" I said. "Oh no, I hardly know you! We're not even dating!"

"But I love you," he said.

So I said, "Look, you're so sweet, and I really will treasure this moment always, just as I treasure your friendship. But no, I can't marry you. I just don't feel the same way." He was crushed, I mean mortally wounded, and somehow surprised, it seemed. I felt horrible about the whole thing, too.

Years later, I saw him and he acted like a nice old friend who'd forgotten all that, but the truth is, his proposal basically ended our friendship. It took a rejected marriage proposal for him to take the hint that I wasn't the one for him.

———

ALL'S WELL THAT ENDS WELL

Maybe you should carry-on (or insure) your luggage next time.

Jennifer Roolf-Laster tells the story of a fateful day in Santa Fe when almost everything went wrong.

The ski trip came as something of a surprise.

"Skiing?" I asked him. "I've never been."

Growing up in San Antonio, it's not the kind of sport you engage in. But Brant, whom I had been dating for almost three years, grew up out in far West Texas, only a few hours away from the mountains of New Mexico. He and his friends would go for weekend ski trips all the time, and he missed the thin, brittle air of the mountains and the feel of the snow, slippery and solid, beneath his skis.

We planned a long weekend to Santa Fe, a town with art galleries and restaurants aplenty—just in case skiing wasn't my thing. We also invited another couple, so the women could sip hot chocolate in the ski lodge while the men were conquering the slopes.

Brant made the arrangements, and they seemed easy enough. We bought tickets to El Paso, with a connecting flight in Midland. Our friends, who were driving, would pick us up in El Paso, where we'd all share the road trip through the mountains.

It wasn't quite so simple.

At the airport, we checked our luggage straight through to El Paso and boarded our plane to Midland.

It was delayed. Considerably delayed.

By the time we made it to Midland, we had missed the connecting flight to El Paso.

Our luggage, however, had made it.

I still don't understand how this happened. But it did. While we stood in the Midland Airport, surrounded by hundreds of other people in the same situation, our luggage merrily winged its way on to El Paso. We tried to catch a later flight on to El Paso to catch up with our luggage.

No luck.

"I'm afraid we only fly to El Paso twice a day," the agent told us. "You'll have to wait another eight hours for the next flight. Or, wait. . ." He kept scrolling down his computer screen. "How about if we fly you straight into Santa Fe? It leaves in 45 minutes, and you'll be there this afternoon."

We jumped at the chance.

Of course, our luggage was not so lucky. The airline was able to tell us it was in El Paso, but they couldn't get it flown out to Santa Fe for several days.

I was not concerned. The luggage wasn't lost, we'd be getting everything back–and this was a chance to go shopping in Santa Fe.

For a West Texan with a laconic attitude and an even more relaxed accent, Brant was freaking. We *had* to have the luggage back, he told the agent. He begged. He implored. He tried to bribe.

It wasn't happening.

Finally, we called our friends that were supposed to pick us up in El Paso and asked if they'd mind picking up just our luggage–not us.

I won't go into the countless phone calls this arrangement necessitated. The airlines had our luggage, and they didn't want to let it go–not to meet with us in Santa Fe and certainly not to be picked up by someone who wasn't even flying with them.

Finally, after signing away what felt like our first-born child, we got it done. Our friends had the luggage, and we had a ticket to Santa Fe.

"It's really the best of all possible worlds," I told Brant, as we settled in for our second flight of the day. "We'll be there early, can rent a car, and just go explore a bit on our own. It'll be fine."

You won't believe me when I tell you there was not a single car for rent in Santa Fe that day. We called our friends who were driving in from El Paso again. "Would you mind picking us up?"

They did, but what could they say? It was going to be several more hours while we waited for them.

We proceeded to the airport bar to put in our time.

Altitude sickness is not something I even knew existed before, but after one glass of wine, I discovered it. The details don't bear repeating, but I was violently ill, with no change of clothes, and there we were stuck in an airport for two more hours.

Santa Fe was fast not becoming my favorite place.

By the time our friends came to pick us up, the sun had set. My clothes, which I'd washed and dried in the airport bathroom, while I guzzled water and Dramamine, had dried, and Brant and I were both beyond exhausted.

When we got to the hotel, they had given away both of our rooms because we were not there at check-in. They had one open room, with two double beds, but that was all.

We wound up at a Best Western, where the sight of the 1980s pink-and-turquoise bedspread was enough to make me weak in the knees. Or maybe it was the Dramamine.

I collapsed on the bed, holding my head, while Brant rummaged through the recovered luggage, making infinitely more noise than I would have liked.

"What a nightmare!" I said. "Thank you for taking care of everything today."

"I will always take care of you," Brant said, "if you'll let me."

As I remember this now, it sounds incredibly cheesy, but at the time, of course, it wasn't. I had my hand over my eyes, trying to block the fluorescent lights that were beaming into my altitude-sickened brain, so I didn't even see the ring until he leaned in to kiss my cheek and nudged my hands out of the way of my eyes.

That was almost eight years ago. We married five months later, and he's been taking care of me ever since.

Except, of course, for when I'm taking care of him.

The first thing I taught him as a married man? Never pack an engagement ring in a bag you're checking-through on an airline.

———

TIMING
IS EVERYTHING

Maybe she just means "not right now," like
Hillary Clinton

It has been reported that President Bill Clinton's marriage proposals were repeatedly rejected when he and Hillary Rodham were dating because she felt the time just wasn't right yet.

In the *Time* magazine article "Hillary Unbound," published on Sunday, June 8, 2003, Senator Hillary Clinton writes, "I was desperately in love with him but utterly confused about my life and future. So I said, 'No, not now.' What I meant was, 'Give me time.'

My mother had suffered from her parents' divorce, and her sad and lonely childhood was imprinted on my heart. I knew that when I decided to marry, I wanted it to be for life . . .

Bill Clinton is nothing if not persistent. He sets goals, and I was one of them. He asked me to marry him again, and again, and I always said no. Eventually he said, 'Well, I'm not going to ask you to marry me any more, and if you ever

> Bill Clinton is nothing if not persistent. He sets goals, and I was one of them.

decide you want to marry me, then you have to tell me.' He would wait me out."

Backing off a bit must have worked. The couple has been married since 1975.

———

The previous stories reiterate some of our rules of engagement: Don't ask a woman unless you know she's going to say yes, and the timing has to be right for her, not just for you. Keep these things in mind, and chances are you won't get "shot down" when you propose.

ADVICE FROM THE EXPERTS

S till not sure how you want to propose? If you have questions, it's always wise to turn to the experts. Call a hotel concierge or hotel public relations representative and ask what has been done at their hotel properties, as they may be able to give you ideas. Or call a local wedding-coordinator and ask what her brides and grooms may have done in the past that was especially memorable. Ask pastors, priests, and rabbis about couples they have married and how those proposals were handled. Even better would be to ask happily married men how they did it, and what they suggest.

If you don't have time for that, then read on. We did some of the leg work for you and called upon a few experts of our own for some final advice regarding the rules of engagement and proposals.

ROMANCING THE STONE

Wedding consultant advice for proposal setting and ring purchase

California-based wedding consultant Maria Lindsay, of Maria Lindsay Wedding and Event Planning of Laguna Beach, offers this advice to today's grooms-to-be:

"The bottom line is romance and red roses. Do something really romantic. Guys try for these wild and contemporary proposals these

> "Buy the main stone you want her to wear for the rest of her life, and then maybe go together to pick out the setting."

days, and that's fine, but the bottom line is that it has to be extremely, drippingly romantic. I've heard that The Ritz-Carlton hotels will do special things, as I'm sure most fine hotels do. They prepare it all for you, and they have a table waiting with chocolate-covered strawberries and champagne—the kinds of things that women think are just to die for. You see, when it gets to the nitty gritty and it's time to propose, remember that the basic romantic things that they'll really remember and rave about in the end are mainly just a beautiful ring and a very romantic proposal," says Lindsay.

When asked if the prospective bridegroom has to have a ring when he proposes, Lindsay's answer is a definitive "Yes!"

" . . . Oh, most definitely! These days, a lot of the gentlemen will buy the main stone and put it on just what we call a doughnut band, or just a very simple basic ring, and then he'll tell the bride that she can go out and select the setting she wants for the stone. That's the smart thing to do. Buy the main stone you want her to wear for the rest of her life, and then maybe go together to pick out the setting." Shopping for a ring setting together is something she'll enjoy, and she'll get the ring she always wanted, but you'll have already surprised her with the "rock."

PROPOSE IN THE MOONLIGHT

On the Beach at Amelia Island Plantation

Amelia Island Plantation Resort, on a beautiful barrier island in northern Florida, is used to hosting world-class wedding events, and so the staff there has seen their share of romantic proposals. The hotel is more than ready to accommodate any requests—no matter how unusual or "over the top"—for the prospective bridegroom as he prepares to pop the question.

Michelle Guglielmo-Gilliam, public relations manager for Amelia Island Plantation, offers these suggestions for some possible romantic proposals.

"A guy could take his bride to dinner and then take a moonlight stroll along the three-and-a-half miles of beach here on our property at the resort. About a mile down the beach, we can arrange to have a romantic candle-lit table for two on a secluded spot on the sand at the edge of the waves, with roses, champagne, chocolate covered strawberries—anything she'd like. Tiki torches could light the path to the table. We could arrange to have someone there to serenade them, or a violinist, or they could just be alone, if they prefer. The man and his girlfriend could 'accidentally' stumble onto this table, and there, a little ring box could be waiting on the center of a china plate, in a glass of champagne, or on top of a chocolate truffle. Again, we can accommodate whatever the guy requests. We can even have 'Will you marry me?' written in the sand so she sees that as they're strolling along the beach hand in hand with the waves of the Atlantic lapping at their feet."

Or, if the couple is really into sports—golf, tennis, kayaking, or whatever—the staff at Amelia Island says they can help to arrange a proposal on the golf or tennis course.

"The ring could be in a box on the final hole on the golf course, or it could be in a tackle box if they like to fish on the end of a pier. Some couples like to take nature hikes on our 1,350-acre property. We have seven miles of trails, so there are lots of secluded, beautiful spots to stop along the way and propose. There is a lovely church on the property, not far from the nature trails, too, and that might be a touching place for a proposal," says Guglielmo-Gilliam.

"Or a guy could set up a couple's massage and spa treatment and propose to his girlfriend there. Of course, we can have a room all ready to surprise her, perhaps our Presidential Suite or Honeymoon Suite, and there waiting for the couple can be champagne and roses on a table with fine linens and crystal and candlelight on the balcony overlooking the ocean, or rose petals on the bed or in the bath. Whatever the groom-to-be thinks might be most romantic, we can arrange it for him," says Guglielmo-Gilliam. "At Amelia Island Plantation, we pride ourselves on our service as well as on our fabulous property. My advice to guys who want to propose to their girlfriends at a destination resort would be to call them in advance so it will be simply perfect when that special day comes."

———

GET ME TO THE CHURCH ON TIME

Make your proposal a sacred moment in a sacred place

If you, or your bride, is religious, another romantic place to propose might be a church or synagogue. Asking a woman to marry you in a place as peaceful and sacred as a church or synagogue is a testament to the seriousness with which you take this commitment—a sign to her that you want to make sure that your relationship with one another is based on a relationship with God, too.

———

FINAL ADVICE FROM *FINAL DESTINATION II* STAR MICHAEL LANDES

Remember, You're Marrying Into a Family

Michael Landes, the good-looking and happily married star of the David Kelly sitcom *The Wedding Bells* (Fox) has starred in movies such as *Final Destination II*, *Hart's War*, and *Dream for an Insomniac*, as well as on television shows, including *Special Unit 2*, *CSI Miami*, *Lois and Clark*, *The Wonder Years*, and others. Landes met his wife, actress Wendy Benson, on the set while starring in and producing *The Gentleman from Boston*.

Landes' latest series, *The Wedding Bells*, is set in a wedding palace, where he is the photographer working with three wedding planners for high-end California nuptial events.

Landes and Benson had to deal with a bi-coastal courtship, as she was filming another movie with Mickey Rourke at the time, so it took awhile before the couple could be in the same place long enough to enjoy their relationship without worrying about airports, taxis, and movie sets. When Landes was finally ready to propose, the actor asked her father, famed *Vanity Fair* photojournalist Harry Benson, if he might have Wendy's hand in marriage. Landes says that asking the dad is very important, and so he offers this advice to today's grooms-to-be:

"You're going to be part of her family for the rest of your life, so it is very important that you respect and honor that family enough to ask for their blessing before you propose. I know I was so nervous that I could hardly talk to Wendy's dad, and even though I was spending Christmas with her family, it took me until the last day to get the nerve to finally ask him. But in the end, it was the right thing to do. It meant a lot to him, and to Wendy's mother, Gigi, but most of all, it meant a lot to Wendy. It also paved the way for a good, respectful relationship with the family that has only grown closer and deepened over the years."

Landes adds, "We have two children now, and when it's time for my daughter, Mimi, to get married, I would hope that the man she loved would respect me enough to ask for my daughter's hand, too."

"Of course, I'm going to make the guy sweat and say 'no,' though. No one's going to be good enough for my baby!" he says with a grin.

———

However you decide to propose, be sure that you enjoy the moment too.

Remember, "Will you marry me?" may be the most important question you'll ever ask in life. So go ahead: Trust your instincts. Trust your love. It's going to be fine. Walk the line.

PART THREE

START PLANNING YOUR WEDDING

· 12 ·

WHAT YOU ARE IN FOR

So you've made it. You bought your rock and presented it in such a memorable way that your new fiancée doesn't miss an opportunity to brag about your proposal to anyone who will listen. What an exciting time in your life. But now what? Sit back, relax, grab a tux here, pay for a few flowers there, enjoy the well-deserved bedroom rewards for such a great proposal, and eventually get married, right?

Yes, you should be relaxed and definitely reap the rewards of your proposal, but you do have a responsibility and role in your wedding planning beyond "just showing up." It's been said that girls dream of a wedding their whole lives, while marriage just happens to men. Because you're reading this book, we can assume that you are not into this assumption. There are some big changes ahead, and it's great that you are taking the time to learn about those changes so that the transition from bachelor to husband is as smooth as possible.

Before we get to the topic of wedding planning, we felt it was necessary to spend a chapter talking about your relationship with your new fiancée and how it changes during engagement. We like to compare the engagement period to the peak of the first hill on the roller coaster. You're picking up speed and headed toward some crazy turns and loops up ahead. These bumps are going to be different for everyone, but you'll surely experience them. "It's not uncommon for people to go through a variety of

> What could possibly be disruptive when everything feels so right? The truth is, a lot.

emotions upon coming engaged," says Gregory Kuhlman, Ph.D., of Brooklyn College, City University of New York. "[P]eople are different, but everybody goes through some degree of anxiety."

Dr. Kuhlman is the director of the Personal Counseling Program at Brooklyn College, where he is also a psychology professor. He and his wife Patricia started the Marriage Success Training program. We turned to Dr. Kuhlman when putting this book together because of his expertise in both the psychology and marriage fields. We wanted to know what couples think and feel during the engagement process and how it differs from couple to couple.

Most likely, if it's early on in your engagement, you are looking at your relationship and thinking you have nothing to worry about. You're finalizing plans for you and your soul mate, who you obviously know really well. The wedding plans have been going smoothly, you're still in a glow over this important next step, and there's nothing but a laundry list of positives ahead. What could possibly be disruptive when everything feels so right? The truth is, a lot.

The reason we don't say, "what could go wrong," is that it's not necessarily *wrong* to experience stress between you and your fiancée in the upcoming months or years preceding your marriage. If handled well, stress can actually make your relationship stronger.

In today's world, with dual-career families and changes in social norms, more couples are living together before they get married. Many consider it a good opportunity to "practice their marriage" in a setting where there is a little more flexibility and a little less pressure. By the time engagement and marriage roll around, they will have already had some time to test the waters. He can get used to her clutter in the bathroom, and she can train him to put the toilet seat down. Many people believe that this time together will lessen the chances of a divorce or breakup once marriage or a more permanent plan is arranged. The truth of the matter is that living together doesn't lower the risk of the relationship going sour at all.

We're not saying you can't live together. By all means, you can get a place and try to convince those in-laws that you sleep on the couch every night. It's all up to the two of you. Just be aware that new issues will arise after the two of you become hitched.

There is a marked difference between dating and your "practice run." Actual marriage is not just a bunch of legal jargon in the court records and a name change. There will be a whole new set of challenges that will require a whole different husband-wife effort. Take finances, for example. Your fiancée may love to go shopping whenever she gets a chance. Maybe you're not a fan, but it doesn't bother you that much. She's in a good mood, which puts you in a good mood. She probably has a job that provides the cash to cover her spending habits. Once you're married, however, it's a different story. You may or may not decide to combine your incomes or share all financial responsibilities. But the spending habit that she brings to the altar becomes a habit that both of you have a say in once the vows are made. In other words, her bills are now, legally, both of your bills, regardless of how you as a couple structure your finances. Her credit history could impact your credit history.

Handling money is just one of the many issues that is about to come up. Dr. Kuhlman believes there are some common issues, or the "big four" as he calls them, which couples worry about during this time. They are:

- Finances
- In-laws
- Kids
- Sex life

These issues may have taken a back seat while you've been dating, but now that marriage is on the horizon, they will have to be confronted. "These are not romantic discussions, but necessary discussions," says Dr. Kuhlman. "The last thing the couple needs is to be blindsided by how much debt their partner is bringing into the marriage."

You'll also be handling a whole new set of emotional challenges. These challenges, along with your day-to-day lives and the added cost of planning a wedding, will undoubtedly cause some stress. There will be plenty of negative times, disagreements, and some unexpected changes in emotions, behavior, and, yes, even your sex life. Knowing and expecting this will be half the battle.

"There are plenty of things that are going to be out of control in your life," says Dr. Kuhlman. "If you want to have any hope of being able to control what happens to you and where your marriage goes, you have to be assertive, you have to be proactive." Being proactive with these issues is going to take a direct conversation with your partner. With Dr. Kuhlman's words in mind, let's take a look at each issue and throw out some questions to start the conversation.

FINANCES

As mentioned previously, after marriage you are no longer two separate people. You are bound together like one complete entity. You may also see it as one credit card bill, one debt, one income, one credit history. You may be entering a binding relationship with someone who's spending and or saving habits are probably unknown to you. You're getting to know each other more and more; how about getting intimate with her bank statements? Here are a few questions the two of you should be asking each other to get to know one another financially.

1. How are we going to split up our finances? Will our accounts be combined or separate? Will we keep our income separate or combine it? Do we need or want a prenuptial agreement?
2. What does money mean to each of us? Is it something fun to spend and enjoy on the spur of the moment? Or is it something to store away as a means toward a secure future?
3. What debt are you or I bringing into this marriage? Do you have credit cards? What are your statements like? On average,

do you pay off your bills immediately or over longer periods of time? What do you or I need help paying off?

4. What do we want to save for in the future and how are we going to achieve that? Are we planning to buy a house in the future? Should we begin retirement funds? If we are to have children, should we start saving for college now?

5. Are we both going to work? Who has the better insurance coverage?

Depending on what you discover during this process, you may want to consider a prenuptial agreement. Before you dismiss this as something meaningless or reserved for high society, know that prenuptial agreements have practical purposes. "People have this notion that they don't mean anything," says Stanford Lotwin of Blank Rome LLP in New York. "I don't know where that notion came from, but they're wrong." As a prominent matrimonial attorney, with clientele like Donald Trump and other high power celebs, Lotwin has seen his fair share of prenuptial agreements under fire. The following explanation will give you a better understanding of prenups and how they offer protection:

"As soon as you're married, you immediately have something called the right of election, which simply means instead of taking what your spouse leaves you in his/her will, you elect to take your statutory share," says Lotwin. "In English, that means whatever the statute in that state provides as a minimum." In some states, this can be as high as one-third or one-half of your estate. Without a prenup in place to say otherwise, your spouse has the right to whatever the government says is fair. So, if after only one month, a skydiving trip proves fatal and your will divides your estate between your new wife and your three kids from a previous marriage equally, she can use her right to elect the statutory minimum. Your children may fight over the other half. Other examples Lotwin has seen include a business owner pushing his partner to get a prenup to protect his share; a family wanting to protect future inheritance; and busy professionals wishing to preserve their personal invest-

PRENUP ADVICE

If you are looking to get a prenuptial agreement, here are some quick steps to follow:

- First off, this is a very important issue that needs to be handled sooner rather than later. You do not want to run into a situation where your fiancée doesn't have an adequate amount of time to think it over or isn't in the right frame of mind to think through the conditions. Emotionally, you want to have this question resolved before you walk down the aisle. Talk it over well in advance of the wedding and allow time for things to cool down, if necessary.

- After talking it over, look for a matrimonial attorney in your area. You can search for these attorneys across the U.S. through the American Academy of Matrimony Attorneys.

- Arrange for a consultation, in which your attorney should explain to you and your fiancée the dangers and implications of a divorce without a prenuptial agreement.

- Make a determination as to how you want to limit or eliminate rights. How will the estate be divided? Who will have a say? Who will pay for counsel fees in the event of a divorce?

- Finally, have your fiancée hire her own attorney to review and work with her independently of you, your family, business partner, or attorney. This is called independent counsel.

ment in a career from a bitter divorce. Lotwin also claims he is seeing more and more brides wanting a prenuptial agreement, which can be easier to take for the groom. "They're normally easy when it's the woman who wants the agreement because the man 'doesn't want anything from you.' It's the macho approach."

Of course, this topic has the potential of being an instant turn-off, so approach your fiancée carefully and respectfully with the idea if you are interested. This might be a conversation that you walk into with full gear and pads on. Very often, discussions surrounding prenuptial agreements can seem like a lack of commitment or belief in the relationship. Truthfully, if you are looking for a prenuptial agreement, there is no benefit conferred to your partner. After all, it gives her less in divorce than if you had married without the agreement. You must be prepared for this response, but know where you are coming from and the practical reasons for wanting one.

IN-LAWS

You've got new relationships with the family on the horizon. They've been a huge influence on her life and suddenly, they're knocking on your door. You may be close with her family, but even so, the extent and nature of your interactions with them is likely to change once you're engaged, and again once you're married. Now that you're a part of two families, it's time to start managing these relationships.

This may also be a good time to discuss whether your fiancée will take your last name or keep her family name. "For some couples this is an easy issue, but for a lot of couples, this is a tough one," says Dr. Kuhlman. Over time, the standards and norms in the U.S. regarding family names have changed and evolved. The tradition of taking the husband's name is not as strong as it used to be. In modern times, there's no set way of doing it.

Be understanding of the reasons your fiancée may have for keeping

Q & A: IN-LAWS

- Which matters in our relationship are public and which are private when talking to the family? Is talking about our financial situation or our sex life off limits to our family, or will we be open?
- How will we split up holidays/vacations between the families? Do we need a predictable routine, or will we decide one occasion at a time?

- What kind of help may we be able to offer to our families if needed in the future?
- What kind of access do our families have? Do rules need to be established regarding visits?
- When we have a problem with a family member, who will be responsible to say something? Is it handled together, or by just one of us?

her name. A woman who is well established in a career may feel that a name change at this point would be detrimental. If that career involves politics, it may be advantageous to use the maiden name, if it is already grounded in the political field, or to use both names, such as Hilary Rodham Clinton does. If your spouse has children from a previous marriage, she may choose to keep her name the same as theirs.

There are plenty of options if you and your fiancée decide not to go the traditional route. You could combine both your names, with or without hyphenation. Your spouse might opt to adopt her maiden name as a middle name. Some wives even take the husband's name, but retain their maiden name professionally. Many times, the bride does not want to go through the hassle of legally changing her name on documents ranging from checks and business cards to mortgages and property deeds. Remember to keep communication open. There's no one way that is right for everyone.

KIDS

For many couples, marriage is a conscious step towards building a family. And by family, we don't mean the new dog you've been thinking about. We're talking about children of your own. Many couples put off the "children" conversation until far too late in the relationship. If kids are in your future, near or far, then you've got plenty to talk about.

Q & A: KIDS

- If we have children, who will be the primary caregiver?
- How many children should we have? If we plan to have more than one, how far apart should we have them?
- What kind of financial arrangements have we made or will we need to make for their future? Should we begin college savings?
- What kind of discipline can we agree on? Who will be responsible for the discipline?
- What schools would we like our children to be in?

SEX LIFE

This is often the largest worry among grooms-to-be, so we've saved this issue for last. "Is this the last woman I will ever have sex with?" or "What if the sex loses its appeal and begins to fade right after marriage?"–these are some very common, even if fleeting, concerns that you will probably face, if you haven't already. And they're worth thinking about—let's not forget this is a huge commitment.

The sex life issue and related worries can be cured with plenty of good communication between you and your partner. Realizing the taboo that surrounds it (really, who's willing to discuss the intimate details of their sex lives? Show of hands, please), we've consulted the renowned "loveologist," Dr. Ava Cadell, or, as she's more popularly known, Dr. Ava. A certified sexologist, doctor of philosophy and education in human sexuality, author of seven books, and television regular on networks from CNN to MTV, Dr. Ava knows the ins and outs of any variety of sex life. "I think one of the biggest fears most men have is that once they get married, sex will diminish; they'll be trapped; that the wife will become a homely wife instead of a seductress girlfriend," she says. Again, she stresses proper communication. "We can't read each other's minds. Knowledge is power and sexual knowledge is sexual satisfaction," she says. "What turned you on when you were dating? You have to say I want my sex life to still be as exciting as it was." Dr. Ava adds that women can be led to think that they no longer have to seduce their husband because now they've successfully got him. Whose fault is it if you are not seduced? "If you don't tell her how important it is to you, then you can't blame her for being lazy."

Q & A: SEX LIFE

- What do you like sexually? What were you into when you were dating? What would you like to try?
- Boundaries and deal breakers: What's off limits that you absolutely will not try?

- What is your idea of fidelity?
- Can I have friends of the opposite sex?
- With these friends, what interactions are acceptable and what are unacceptable?

Dr. Ava says that you and your partner should define specifically where your sexual boundaries are. Not doing so may create some residual resentment or hope that these techniques may be later used.

Still worried about your late-night future? Beyond talking it out, Dr. Ava offers some additional approaches to keep your sex life interesting:

DR. AVA'S TOOLS FOR FULFILLING SEX

■ **A Wish List.** Compose a wish list of the things you would like to do with your partner sexually. This list can include anything and everything within your discussed boundaries. Then, together with your partner, work to make these wishes come true on a regular basis. As Dr. Ava suggests, "Every month, they should make three wishes come true." This will ensure that there will be some variety in your sex life—falling into a rut will be more difficult.

■ **A Pleasure Log.** Different styles of communication often make it difficult to know when one's significant other is "in the mood." Face it, even if we were psychics, when it starts getting hot, our minds tend to go into autopilot. A pleasure log is a notebook or a diary that keeps track of the things that give you both pleasure. Jot ideas down whenever they come up or when you are particularly "inspired."

■ **Mission Statement.** "I think it's important to write a couple's mission statement, expressing your goals. Display it somewhere where you

(continued)

(continued from p109)

can see it on a regular basis." Write what outlines your sexual life and your sexual relationship. What does your sex life demand? What are some long-term goals you have? Maybe you want to be regular with your partner for the next 20 years. Maybe you need public displays of affection every once in a while. This way, if things start to take a turn for the worse, you've got your own "bible of the bedroom." Remember to keep what's important to your sex lives in focus.

■ **Exchange Roles of Power.** Another way to avoid falling into a rut in your sex life is to take turns: Make sure that the same person is not the initiator every single time. An exercise that Dr. Ava came up with involves blindfolding your partner and making love to them blindfolded. "[W]hen you make love to your partner who is blindfolded, you lose all your inhibitions."

It's simple logic, guys: Most men are concerned about the quantity in their sex life. Women, on the other hand, tend to be concerned about the quality of their sex life. These aren't contradicting points, however. Work to improve the quality of her sex life, and she'll want more. In other words, concentrate on her needed quality and you won't have time to sleep. Everyone's a winner and victory was never so "stimulating."

If you're a couple that has decided to abstain from sex before marriage, there are still plenty of related issues to consider during this time. Engagement is a time of anticipation for both you and your partner to begin to enjoy a new level of sexuality in your relationship. What can you do to keep the affection alive while such anticipation is building, without deviating from the plan? The answer, according to Dr. Ava, is simple: "Everything but intercourse."

She explains the five levels of touch that are essential in a relationship. The first is caring. This could involve holding hands and/or a massage. Second is the romantic touch, involving kissing or petting of the hair. Third, seductive touch is close to foreplay and can involve stimulation without penetration. Fourth is intimate touch, bringing your partner to climax without penetration. The last is intercourse, involving penetration. Depending on your definitions of sex, keep the levels within your boundaries. Another suggestion is to learn tantric lovemaking. "Tantra basically opens up the whole spiritual side of sex," Dr. Ava says. "It incorporates breathing together and making sounds and moving together—it's very loving, very respectful." Books and classes are widely available on the subject. She also adds, "Once you become a really advanced tantra lover, it can open up a whole new world of multiple orgasms." What's not to love about that?

All in all, be open and communicate. Whether you simply sit down and talk about it at the kitchen table or start after you've rolled around on the kitchen table, your sex life will continue to be interesting and exciting if you work together. You might even discover some new moves in the process!

In our talks with Dr. Kuhlman, one theme became crystal clear. The way relationships are built and maintained have changed a lot over the past several years. Traditions that once provided an easy answer for many decisions couples face, such as taking the husband's name or who will be the primary caregiver, are no longer definitive solutions. For these decisions and many like them, as Dr. Kuhlman repeated, "There's not one right way; there are fifteen ways you could do it, so you have to arrive at an agreement."

When you are negotiating, you must understand that you cannot expect to control and/or change your partner.

Take for example, the cleanliness in which we

> Simply knowing that you don't have to follow established rules or norms can do wonders for your relationship.

live. Maybe you don't think twice about tossing your dirty clothes on a growing pile at the foot of the bed, while she can't sleep if there's a shirt on the wrong hanger in the closet. Now, society would have you believe that you are wrong. The person who is neat, clean, and organized is right, correct?

If you choose to be less neat, your partner should not expect you to keep every area clean. Maybe you should have a designated space (such as an office or den) that you can keep how you like. If you work best in a less-than-tidy environment, then for you it may be right.

Try another example: punctuality. You like to arrive at an appointment with time to spare, whereas your fiancée takes the liberty of showing up 10 or 15 minutes late. Society would have you believe that punctuality is the proper way, right? But then there are times when it's appropriate to be "fashionably late." In some cultures, if you show up on time for anything, you end up waiting around for at least an hour. It's important in negotiating these issues to understand that the norms of your family or your upbringing or your personality are not the only "right" ways for the two of you to live. With this in mind, you're ready to start the process.

KEYS TO COMMUNICATION

1. **Schedule a time to negotiate.** It's good to be able to address a problem together with as few distractions as possible. "[M]ake an appointment together when you're both well-rested and when you're both feeling more resilient and not feeling overloaded from your job," says Dr. Kuhlman. If this particular issue or a couple of issues are chronic, you may want to schedule an appointment every week. Make sure not to talk about the issue outside of the allotted time.

2. **Be positive.** Do not bring up the situation in

a critical or attacking tone. If this is how you approach it, you're begging for a fight, and no constructive outcomes can be reached. Many will find that it's difficult to settle who will do the dishes when your fiancée is throwing them at you.

3. **Take a break if needed.** Often, one person is more prone to "overload," a term the experts have coined for the "drinking water out of a fire hydrant" types— those who demand too much too fast. Overload occurs when a person pushes a disagreement, causing it to escalate too quickly into an argument. This often results in the other person shutting down mentally or physically from a negotiation. As Dr. Kuhlman explains, typical disagreements and negotiations follow a model. One person will be more prone to overload and the other will tend to withdraw, or remove his or herself from the discussion. Seeing the other partner withdraw, the person prone to overload will push the issue even more. On average, the men tend to withdraw while the females are inclined to engage more. "She doesn't know why he's reacting this way and she takes it personally. And it's not. You get this way and it becomes a vicious cycle. They feel they're stuck in this script," says Dr. Kuhlman. If you find yourself in this situation, agree to take a break. Give yourselves twenty minutes or so to cool off; chances are you'll come back to the discussion with new patience and perspective.

Be proactive.
You've got plenty of new issues coming your way. Now is the time to talk about them.

Negotiate. Know your boundaries and deal-breakers, but accommodate for each other and both of your choices.

Communicate and be specific.
You can't read one another's minds, and unless you both keep diaries and occasionally steal a look, you'll never know what your partner is missing in your relationship or vice versa. Keep her informed, and stay updated on her views.

You're probably wondering why, in addition to your meetings at work, you now have to schedule meetings with your soul mate and take time-outs. This model might seem artificial at first, but many couples who use it find that it saves them from a lot of dead-end arguments, and that eventually they can communicate easily without thinking about the structure at all.

When asked what the key ingredients to marital success are, Dr. Kuhlman gives three answers. First, keep it positive. Experts have even quantified this piece of advice. Imagine your relationship on a spectrum or scale. One side of the scale is positive, the other side is negative. To make your relationship successful, you must have five positive interactions for every negative one. Studies have concluded that even slightest differences, such as 4.9 to 1, create a downward trend.

Secondly, make time for the two of you. "[T]o stay bonded, to stay in a satisfied state, [couples] need to spend a minimum of twelve hours of non-sleep, non-TV time together. This can be very difficult during the work week, so that means you really have to plan," says Dr. Kuhlman.

Finally, don't create unrealistic expectations. Don't make your relationship an impossible task or some unattainable treasure. Accommodate for the both of you. After all, your relationship is give and take—a group effort. And if it's meant to be, it will be worth everything you put into it.

———

TIPS

1. **Understand** that not everything is smooth sailing after you propose—problems, stress, and disagreements are bound to appear. Many of the problems may come from situations you were never exposed to in your dating days.

2. **Be proactive.** Sit down with your partner and discuss problematic areas: finances, in-laws, sex life, and children if need be. These conversations aren't romantic, but proactive discussion will help you two address the problems as they come up.

3. **Communication is key.** A large part of being proactive is communicating your worries, feelings, et cetera, to your partner. Don't let the issues or emotions between you and your fiancée remain a guessing game as the countdown continues towards the big day.

4. **Negotiate.** When you do have your discussions, be prepared to negotiate. Recognize whether or not you need to take a break if tensions run high. Give it time, be patient, and the compromises will come.

5. **Keep things positive** and create time for the both of you. You're on the verge of a large commitment. Start it up right.

· 13 ·

THE GROOM'S JOB

Now that you're mentally prepped, its time to step out of the dugout and into the trenches. Wedding planning might not be a man's forte. But you're going to learn, and you're going to have to learn fast. This is all part of the deal.

If you think that your fiancée has been dreaming of every little detail of this wedding her whole life, you're probably right. However, this doesn't mean that she should run the show all on her own. She's probably been dreaming of you being an active participant, too. Planning your wedding should be a team effort, an opportunity for you to create an event together that reflects your personality as a couple.

Most likely, being a passive participant in the planning will only create more problems for you. If you try to hand off the responsibility of the wedding to your detail-oriented and seemingly perfectionist fiancée, you're practically handing her a second, full-time job. Don't expect her to be grateful for that plan.

So be an active participant. There are plenty of aspects of the wedding planning that are traditionally or popularly reserved for the groom, such as the groom's dinner, the music, alcohol, and transportation. While maybe not as visible as the cake or flower arrangements, these decisions are still an integral part of the wedding. We've compiled the portions of the planning in which grooms are most typically involved, but again, don't use this as an excuse to get out of picking centerpieces if your fiancée wants your input.

WEDDING PLANNERS

When you start to talk about your wedding, your fiancée will probably want to drag you to a wedding planner. Now, although we guys tend to be do-it-yourselfers, give this some consideration. Think of him or her as a consultant. You'll sit down with your consultant and try to describe, to the best of your abilities, the desired feel and look of your wedding. The consultant then will make recommendations for each part of the event based on your personalities, wants, and wishes. Wedding planners have all the proper contacts to match every requested detail on your list. He or she then becomes a manager, supervising everyone involved–including the two of you–making sure that everything is on time and no detail is overlooked. You don't want to be juggling all of these responsibilities. As famed wedding consultant Frank J. Andonoplas says, "You turn to a professional to get your car done, why would you not turn to a professional to design your wedding?"

Andonoplas is a personality-at-large in the wedding planning business. For fifteen years, his Chicago-based business has coordinated everything from tiny church basement weddings to an elaborate wedding on a boat. Named a "master bridal consultant" by the Association of Bridal Consultants, he has appeared regularly on television networks such as NBC and CBS, and has offered his advice in the *Chicago Tribune* and the *Los Angeles Times* and in magazines including *Bride* and *Modern Bride*. In other words, having Andonoplas plan your wedding compares to hitting balls at batting practice with Babe Ruth.

For Andonoplas, wedding planning is often more than simply managing the event; it is about managing emotions. "I play referee a lot. I've had mothers and daughters fight over chairs before," he says. There is a lot to be done, possibly in addition to you and your fiancée's regular jobs, and tempers are likely to flare. While your fiancée and mother or mother-in-law are not expected to get in disagreements, it's just another thing that Andonoplas is prepared for; he's ready to calm the waters when fights erupt over centerpieces.

Here are some tips from Andonoplas on how to work effectively with your wedding planner:

WEDDING PLANNER WISDOM

- **Be open.** Most wedding planners will take everything into consideration, to best match your style and personality. "I ask clients to give me three words to describe what their wedding will be like. I also have them look through my portfolio and watch very closely for their reactions," he says. After all, this is a very personal event.

- **Be honest.** Don't lowball your wedding planner. Even with the best poker face, the planner is going to know. So although you may be ready to tell your planner you're only going to spend $15,000 and feed, entertain, and serve drinks to 350 people, your planner will know better. This is probably your first wedding plan-

ning experience. However, your planner has probably managed many weddings this year, maybe even hundreds, and unless you can beat that, there's not a poker face in the world that could convince him or her that you know better than he or she does.

- **Trust your planner.** He or she knows the contacts and how things will, or should, turn out. Andonoplas has done a wedding with only three weeks notice, but his clients had to follow his lead religiously, allowing him to make most of the decisions. While you don't have to take all of a planner's suggestions, be open and give his or her recommendation some serious thought.

12 to 18 Months Ahead

Book a reception hall

FIRST THINGS FIRST

This is truly a jovial time in your life. Before your emotions carry you into the cake shop, let's get some priorities straight. You're on an agenda.

"The first thing you need to do is decide when and where. You can't do anything until that is done," says Andonoplas. "You need to decide how many people you are going to invite and how much you are going to spend." These are the foundations to lay before you start making any other plans. Once you've chosen the date, you can inquire to see whether or not your location will be available. When you've decided how many people you want to invite, then you can check to see if your reception hall will hold that many, making changes if necessary.

Often, reception halls are booked months in advance, especially for desirable special dates, such as Valentine's Day. Andonoplas recommends that a proper range for planning is somewhere between 12 and 18 months.

You also need to set the budget. Don't even think about ordering food or renting a limo before you have a ballpark figure. If your parents or in-laws are helping out with the costs, know how much they are willing to spend and figure that in. Allow yourselves to dream, but realize that there have to be boundaries. Set limits early to prevent debt nightmares later.

Once you've laid these foundations, you're ready to move ahead.

EVENTS

While the actual wedding requires plenty of forethought and scheduling, there are other events surrounding the big day that also need to be planned. Most commonly, these four other events include:

1. Engagement Party
2. Groom's Dinner
3. Bachelor Party
4. Honeymoon

Engagement party

Your engagement party celebrates your engagement with family and close friends and properly introduces the two families to each other. Traditionally, the engagement party is the responsibility of the bride's family. Now, however, it's not uncommon to have the engagement party hosted by a close friend or the groom's family. Geography will probably be the determining factor for location: choose some place that will be the most accommodating for everyone. If you and your fiancée live together and your family lives down the street, while hers lives across the state, it might not be the best choice to pack everyone in the van and travel 300 miles for the sake of tradition and a meal. At the same time, be careful not to step on anyone's toes. If her family is very excited about hosting a gala dinner for the both of you and your family, then don't let your friend Beau think he can throw a beer and chips bash at his bachelor pad instead.

While one of the reasons for an engagement party is to allow the families to finally meet, you need not exclude friends from the event. In fact, if any friends are close to both families, it may be a good idea to invite them along to help the families break the ice. Make sure, however, that those who are invited will also be on the wedding guest list. Also, gifts should not be expected. Don't worry—you'll get plenty down the road.

> You can have a fabulous, home-cooked dinner provided by one or both sets of parents, or a lavish five-course evening.

Groom's dinner/Rehearsal dinner

The groom's dinner, or rehearsal dinner, is typically hosted by the groom's family, whether at their house or another venue. This dinner takes place the evening before the wedding, following the run-through of the ceremony. It is your opportunity to thank everyone who has supported and taken part in the ceremony. If you have gifts to give to your bridesmaids and groomsmen (if not, give it some serious thought!), this is the time to give them.

Again, similar to the engagement party, this can be as formal or informal as you want. You can have a fabulous, home-cooked dinner provided by one or both sets of parents, or a lavish five-course evening. Andonoplas has even seen one creative idea in which the couple and their party had a progressive dinner, where they hit up multiple restaurants, having a course at each. So you have many options, all depending on how many will be invited and what your budget for the affair is.

As far as who you have to invite, think of the key players in your ceremony—at least the immediate families of yourself and your bride, plus the wedding party. You may also choose to invite the wedding officiant and his or her spouse, as he or she plays a necessary role and will be working with you before the dinner.

Sometimes couples wonder if they should invite out-of-town guests. It's certainly a nice gesture of appreciation for traveling many miles to partake in the wedding. You'll also be offering them a meal with some familiar folks, instead of letting them fend for themselves in an unfamiliar city or town they just arrived in. This, of course, will factor into your cost. Having a barbeque or potluck will make this gesture more possible, but you could also invite everyone to the bar and provide appetizers or bar snacks.

Some couples choose to split up for the dinner. In this case, the groom's dinner can also serve as an alternative to the bachelor party. Let it be known that there is no tradition that says, "Thou shalt, before thy wedding, get drunk and have risqué experiences with scantily-clad women." You have the "option" of doing this. But we're not the ones granting you the option. Your fiancée is. More on bachelor parties soon.

Instead of a wild night of last-minute, last-time-in-my-life endeavors, the groom's dinner is generally a classier and more mature outing for the guys. Hit up the biggest steakhouse in town and have a couple of drinks with your fathers and best buds.

Whatever sort of groom's dinner you decide on, a little planning and forethought will ensure it's a fun and relaxing opportunity to catch up with your closest friends and family before the flurry of the wedding day activities.

Bachelor party/Stag party

When we think of bachelor parties, we get a flood of images—strippers, plenty of booze, more strippers. Then we think of the angry fiancée.

The bachelor party doesn't have to be about getting so intoxicated that you honestly can't remember it when you wake up the next day. Darren Hitz, founder of Hitz Adventures LLC, offers 30 different adventure packages for a groom's bachelor party. "The real goal is, in two years when you get together, to be able to tell stories. We're putting grooms and their buddies in unique places and creating memories," says Hitz. "Having a good time does not have to involve the risk of a drunken injury or a lifetime of trouble—you don't have to do something

> A weekend adven-
> ture with the guys
> might be much more
> memorable—and
> remembered—than
> a night at the bar.

that you could end up regretting. No one goes on one of my trips and regrets it."

So you may want to examine what you really want to get out of your bachelor party before you start to talk to your best man about it. A weekend adventure with the guys might be much more memorable—and remembered—than a night at the bar. If a weekend of ocean fishing or skydiving seems like a huge task to plan, consider putting the planning in someone else's hands. Hitz's packages cost, on average, $399 per person and include everything: the plane tickets, the trip with the outfitter, lodging, and food. All you'll have to do is pack your bags and show up. Other trips with your buddies that might be easier to plan include a camping/cabin trip, golfing out of state, four-wheeler or snowmobile trips—the list can go as far as your interests take you!

If your heart is set on simply having some drinks with your guy friends in a more risqué situation (maybe that last-chance visit to the strip club), then who is stopping you? And no, that's not just a figure of speech. Really look and recognize what or "who" is stopping you from that plan. Depending on whom you are planning to marry—and you should know best—consider whether this choice will cause ripples in your relationship. She may hate the idea of you guys having your night of mayhem. She might say it's okay and give you that "but you'll regret it" look afterwards. If this is the case, or you suspect so in the least, then really examine your choices. "Nobody can answer those questions for you, but you know your fiancée, you need to put the situation in context. This is right before your wedding. This is not a good time to piss off your partner," says Dr. Kuhlman. "Do you want to be standing up there exchanging vows and gritting your teeth? On the other hand, do you want to be up there exchanging vows, thinking you have to give up the relationship with your buddies?" Your experience at the altar is ultimately more important than your bachelor party, so weigh your options carefully.

8 Months Ahead

Book your honeymoon

Honeymoon

Finally, the honeymoon. We can safely say that most grooms tend to be pretty excited about the honeymoon. Of course, everybody loves a good vacation, and, well, a honeymoon is extra exciting. Years ago, the tradition was to have the wedding consummated right after the ceremony—with witnesses present. After the ceremony, the bride and groom would leave, hoping to evade the crowd and get some privacy. In fact, the cans on the back of a car were used as a makeshift homing device; they were an audible clue as to where the couple was driving to.

Nowadays, the honeymoon is a time to relax and have some intimate time alone with your new spouse, free of any and all distractions. Maybe you've got a tropical island getaway in mind, or a backpacking excursion through Europe. Even if you are not going to some far-away destination, this is an important event and you need to do your homework. Leslie Delorme, a honeymoon specialist from Carlson Wagonlit Travel, says that, on average, it is the bride that comes in to the agency to plan the honeymoon. However, she also notes that, typically, it is the groom who pays for it. So be sure to go in there and have your say.

DELORME'S HONEYMOON PLANNING TIPS:

1. **Plan in advance.**
   Your honeymoon should be planned about eight months in advance.

2. **Know how much you want to spend.**
   Delorme usually sees honeymoons costing around $5,000 or less, but the number really depends on how long and where the honeymoon will be.

3. **Use a travel agent.**
   You're invited to look on your own, but be warned. While a travel agent isn't always the cheapest option, if anything goes wrong along the way, it's much easier to have a travel agent to call on for help.

With all the intense focus on honeymoons and "what they are for," you may be worried about keeping things from being awkward once you arrive. Okay, for most of you, this won't be a problem. But for some of you, you're at risk of opening the door to the hotel room and saying a great liner like this: "Well, we're here. I guess we should, well, 'get to it,' and, you know, do those things that happen on honeymoons?" Wow, let's hope not.

Even so, Dr. Ava Cadell, loveologist, has provided some advice on keeping the mood light. "You have to make it very playful and fun. And that takes the pressure off taking it all too seriously. I would recommend taking some adult toys and massage lotion," she says. After all, she says, sex is just adult play. Go to your honeymoon with the idea of having a good time and getting to know your partner in a new way. Don't stress over or cave into the pressure of having to perform. Rather, build some anticipation. "The more playful, the more foreplay, the more sexual anticipation, the better," says Dr. Ava.

WEDDING DAY DETAILS

Beyond the events that the groom is typically involved in planning or hosting, there are some details on the wedding day itself that the groom usually plans. These typically include:

- Transportation
- Alcohol
- Music
- Tuxedos

TRANSPORTATION

When we talk about transportation, we aren't just talking about how you and your bride travel from the photo shoot to the church to the reception. You might need to arrange for out-of-town guests to be picked up from the airport, or for a van to take guests from a hotel to the wedding and back, so they don't have to worry about driving after consuming alcohol.

Depending on your location, you may have multiple types of transportation to choose from. Popular options include:

- Limo
- Horse-drawn carriage

- Trolley
- Specialty vehicle (such as a Rolls Royce, or rented classic Mustang)
- A relative's classic car or sports car

Some pretty nice options, right? Now, before you start making calls to the company offering stretch Hummers, ask yourself a couple of questions:

1. How many people are you going to be transporting? In other words, if you're hiring limos, how many will you need in order to accommodate the entire wedding party? If you want to pick up out-of-towners, you'll have to figure that in, too. When counting the bride as a passenger, make sure to count her as two people to allow room for her bridal gown. To avoid certain disaster, be sure to make it clear in discussions that you are counting her as one person and her beautiful, flowing gown as another—and not that you are counting her as two people.

2. Do you want a car for just you and your bride, or do you plan to ride with the wedding party? Wedding consultant Andonoplas says, "It's one of the [few] times in the day when you're going to be away from everyone, so I think it's a nice touch [to ride alone]. Away from friends, away from parents—it's a nice time away." But ultimately, it's up to you.

3. How are you going to get the best bang for your buck? Again, that's for "*your* buck." Not for "*a* buck." Look at your budget and see how much you are willing to spend compared to their prices.

4. In your area, on that day, are you going to run into any particular traffic problems? If you are in a large city, will there be any big events/conferences/festivals in the area that will cause traffic to be slowed down to a standstill? Consider such events in other areas of planning as well, as you don't want a professional football game down the road with half-time show F-16s flying

over your ceremony . . . unless you're into that sort of thing.

5. What is the weather typically like at that time of year? If you are doing a spring wedding, you may be running a risk by booking an open-air vehicle. You may really want to go with the horse-drawn carriage, but if it's a freakish winter and snow extends into April, this may not work out so well. Furthermore, if you are doing a summer wedding, how will this affect the vehicle? If you have a classic vehicle, beware of running into overheating problems on a hot summer day.

6. How will you get home or to the hotel at the end of the night? This detail is often forgotten. "A lot of people forget about that," says Andonoplas. "We have brides slipping out of their dresses and getting into a cab—it's funny, a great photo opportunity." Plan for it by extending your transportation booking, or be sure that you can hail a taxi or get a ride from a designated driver.

6 to 8 Months Ahead

Book transportation

Those questions in mind, we'll introduce you to each of the options and their pros and cons, plus offer a price estimate, based on Chicago standards. Be sure to get price rates in your own area before making any decisions. On your timeline, realize that transportation would typically be booked 6 to 8 months in advance.

TRANSPORTATION

- **Limousines.** The obvious choice for weddings. They are classy and stylish, protect you from the elements, and offer the privacy that the President and celebrities enjoy. As far as price and capacity are concerned, these options are relatively middle-of-the-road, costing more than a horse-drawn carriage, but less than a trolley. Typically, for an 8- to 10-passenger limo, you will be charged $125 to $175 per hour.

- **Trolleys.** Offered in the larger metropolitan areas, trolleys can be a great antidote to the common limo. Stylish, often with brass and wooden interiors, you can make quite the old-fashioned entrance to the reception in this vehicle. Trolleys tend to be more expensive than limos, but are able to fit more guests. You can hire a trolley, typically seating 32 passengers, for the required four-hour minimum at $700 to $1,200, or approximately $175 to $300 per hour.

- **Specialty vehicles.** This is a very broad category, ranging from a rented Porsche or Ferrari to a Rolls Royce with chauffeur. You will find most of these options at an exotic rentals dealership. Typically much pricier and with a smaller capacity, these rentals are best suited for a larger budget. Andonoplas warns that some of the specialty vehicles can be problematic, as they require meticulous care and can be affected by the often unpredictable elements.

■ **Horse-drawn carriage.**
An elegant and romantic choice for fall, spring, or summer. You're straight out of a storybook as you're carried to the reception. The capacity and speed can't match its combustion-engine alternatives, but the price can be telling. Carriages typically accommodate four people, and you may be able to book a carriage for $100 to $250 per hour.

■ **A relative's classic car or sports car.** If this is an option for you, it will probably be your cheapest one. However, you might not have the same sense of security or insurance as you would with a professional service. If the hotrod breaks down the night before or during the ceremony, do you have a plan B?

6 Months Ahead

Book a caterer

FOOD/ALCOHOL

The celebration wouldn't be complete without some wining and dining. Everyone has traveled long and far to see you two on your day; now offer them a feast that will fuel them onto the dance floor. You're probably new to ordering food for more than 100 people. Heck, you're probably new to cooking for more than two. Luckily for you, all you have to do is answer some questions and pay the bill.

Depending on where your reception is, a catering staff may be included (all inclusive, most hotels), or you may need to hire an independent catering service. Christine Spearing, Director of Catering/Convention Services at the Omni-Interlocken Resort in Denver, was able to shed some light on what's behind the food and drink at your reception. As for when you should make basic catering decisions, Christine says, "Truthfully, the earlier the better." She recommends six months in advance for proposing an overall idea for what you want, and one month before the wedding to have the caterers or site representatives put it down in writing. They should then give you a date by which you will have to provide a final headcount for each meal. This will typically be from three to five business days before the wedding.

Understand that when deciding what you want to serve, it's more than just what's on the plate. Many times, catering services will have you come in for a tasting, which makes the decision all that much more delicious. You will have to decide other details, such as whether you want the dinner plated (served to guests at their seats) or served in a buffet. The plated dinner adds an elegant touch, but it can be slower than running the crowd through a buffet line. How many pieces (courses/dishes) per person? Pieces could mean an entrée, a salad, an appetizer, a dessert, etc. Typically, three to five pieces is a normal dinner.

Here are some questions that you and your fiancée should decide upon before consulting a caterer: Would you like to have hors d'oeuvres? Do you want a champagne toast? Will you need vegetarian dishes for any of your guests? Make sure to refer to your budget once again.

You should also have some questions for your caterer.

QUESTIONS TO ASK THE CATERER

- What is included in the set-up? China, glass, silver, chairs, tables, centerpieces, cake and/or gift tables?
- What other fees apply? Are there fees for bartenders/staffing? Cake cutting fees? Parking fees?
- Can I bring in food or does it all have to be catered by the facility? If your venue is all-inclusive, you may not be able to get your cake elsewhere, for example.
- What is your overset? Caterers always prepare more spots and dishes than the number you give them in case someone unexpectedly shows up. That number—the overset—is often a percentage of your count.
- How much do you require for a deposit and when is the final payment due?

Spearing's Money-saving Tips

- If you have hors d'oeuvres, order fewer cold and more hot hors d'oeuvres. "People tend to eat more hot."
- Make one of the hors d'oeuvres vegetarian; meatless options are often less pricey.
- Normally, with a 60-person cake, you can get 75 slices; a 100-person cake, 125 slices and so on. "There's a little give in there." However, Spearing warns, "I wouldn't cut that one too close, especially if you want to keep the top. But if it doesn't matter, there's a couple extra slices there." (If you are not familiar with the one-year tradition, it means saving the top layer of your wedding cake to share with your wife on your first anniversary.)

Traditionally, the alcohol at the reception is paid for by the groom or the groom's parents. Some couples choose to have a dry wedding. But if you would like alcohol, there are a lot of creative liquor options for the reception.

First, consider whether you want a cash bar or open bar. A cash bar is where the venue or beverage provider will offer bar, bartender, and a variety of liquors, beers, wines, and non-alcoholic drinks of your choice that your guests will order and pay for. An open or hosted bar provides the same set-up, except all or selected drinks are complimentary for the guests. The venue will run an inventory before and after the reception; whoever is paying the bill, whether the couple, the parents, or a combination of both, pays for the difference. These options aren't black-and-white; depending on the provider, you may be able to bend the rules. Perhaps you would like to have an open bar for cocktail hour and then have a cash bar until the night ends? Or maybe you would prefer to offer beer and house wine to your guests, but you'd rather not pay for the hard alcohol. Either way, it's up to you. Ask your provider what options are available.

Spearing weighs in on the subject. "A combination tends to work better," she says. "From the bride and groom's perspective, people drink less as the time goes by. The first hour or so is going to be the biggest consumption time." Spearing recommends having a hosted bar for the first hour, with the rest of the reception time as either an all-cash bar or a partially hosted bar, with beer and wine complimentary and cash mixed drinks. "I definitely don't recommend [open] bars for more than four hours. From both the bride and groom's perspective and the site's perspective, liability increases dramatically after that."

CREATIVE BAR IDEAS

■ **Signature drinks.** Have one drink, maybe based on the bride or groom's favorite drink, or even the color scheme of the reception. Have stations around the room to make them and or have servers pass them around.

■ **Coffee bar.** Great for both alcoholic and non-alcoholic drinks. Serve the coffee with some Bailey's or Kahlua, or straight with sugar and cream.

■ **Wine bar.** Is your crowd more into wine than beer? Try a wine bar with several varieties to choose from and taste.

■ **Ice luge.** For an interesting visual, find a caterer that will do an ice luge. Carved out of ice, the luge chills the drink as it moves down the ice chute.

If you are looking to save some money, here are several ideas that could help cut the cost of your alcohol bill.

- Check the brands. Is the bar serving top-shelf liquors and expensive wine? Ask for well or call brands instead of top shelf.
- Get a slot price for children. If kids are getting soft drinks (and probably not finishing them) throughout the night, those $4 pops can run your tab unnecessarily.
- Serve a champagne or non-alcoholic punch instead of offering a full bar.
- Cut out mixers and cordials. These are the most expensive items on your alcohol tab.

MUSIC

You've seen them all. The cover band of the couple's favorite 80s rock band, or that DJ that is determined to use the *Chicken Dance* to prod everyone onto the floor. The music can be a huge part of the night's success for your guests. Here you have only a few choices:

- DJ service
- Live band
- Friend's MP3 player

Be aware that these options don't offer the same performance guarantees that the transportation services do. You will probably find tons of offers from unprofessional musicians or DJs with little to no experience. If you have a bunch of music, a computer, and some speakers, you've got yourself a business. If a limo breaks down, in the worst case scenario your guests could give you a ride. If your friend's iPod shorts a circuit, you might as well call it a night. So be warned: you can go with an unprofessional service—you'll undoubtedly save some money—but know that you are taking a large risk.

Before meeting with your DJ or musicians, have a vision of your reception. You'll want to know what you're looking for before you start asking questions of entertainers.

1. **Know your crowd.** If your guests are going to range from young to old, play a variety of music to please everyone. You might like the 1990s grunge scene, but your grandparents never caught onto Nirvana and they want to kick it to a big band. Include them on the dance floor. The last thing you want is an empty dance floor and a bunch of bored guests.

2. **Organization and timing.** How do you want the music to flow? Make sure it builds throughout the night, staying lighter around cocktails and dinner, getting progressively livelier towards the dance portion. Don't jump all over the music spectrum or the ambiance will lose its cohesiveness and feel. A good, experienced entertainer should be able to handle this, if you choose to leave it up to him/her. After all, it's been said that "If you pick the right service, you shouldn't have to pick any song. But if you pick the wrong service, you'll wish you picked every song."

Once you're ready to meet with the DJ or entertainer, here are a few pointers:

1. **Ask for the entertainer's portfolio.** How much experience do they have? How long have they been doing this?

2. **Ask for references.** You may even want to go outside of the entertainer's self-selected references. Often, reception halls observe the DJs or bands at weddings and have an opinion on how they did. If you knew a friend or co-worker who saw them at a wedding, be sure to ask.

3. **Meet them in person.** Sit down and talk with the entertainer face-to-face and make an opportunity to view the equipment. Don't leave anything to speculation.

4. **Do they have liability insurance?** If someone trips over a speaker cable, who is going to be liable for the accident? The DJ? The venue? You?

5. **Ask what happens in the event that the entertainer cannot make it on that day.** People get sick or emergencies occur. Do they have backup DJs or band members on deck to take the gig at a moment's notice? If you are hiring a live band/orchestra/quartet and are shown a movie of a performance, ask if these are the exact group members who will show up for your wedding. If you have your heart set on a particular singer or performer, what will be done in case of his/her absence on that day?

6. **Importantly, you should also ask what music is available.** You may not want to have a band that only plays glam rock if your grandparents are looking to hit the dance floor with a polka. If you want a band to play a specific song, how much will that cost? How much time in advance will they need to teach every member that song?

Music will, in large part, dictate the ambience of your day. Think through your options and make your wishes very clear to whomever you choose.

TUXEDOS

No wedding planning event is complete without the traditional James Bond look-a-like contest. Although we guys don't have the extensive options that the brides do when it comes to apparel, it has never seemed to bother us. The tuxedo has worked for ages, but don't let its simplicity fool you. Choosing correctly is no walk in the park.

You can either buy or rent your tux. While you might toss out the idea of buying a tuxedo based on cost, give it a second thought. Will you have some important formal events in your future with your career or status in the community? Do you project that you'll be in a couple weddings down the road? In this case, buying a tuxedo might be a good investment. Andonoplas agrees, adding, "Hey, she gets a dress."

Buying a tux will cost from $700 to $2,500. Most are in the $1,200 to $1,500 range. You should also know that if you are buying, you will be getting a higher quality product. Not only has it not been rented dozens of times already, but tailors tend to adhere to a higher standard when making a tuxedo for purchase.

Renting a tuxedo will probably cost around $125 to $165, including the shoes. Typically, the tux vendor will throw in the groom's tux rental for free. The groom or the groom's family can pay for all the rentals, but usually, everyone pays for their own tux. Who in the ceremony needs a tux? Your groomsmen and the father of the bride will, almost always, be outfitted in tuxes. Although it's not required, the father of the groom usually wears a tux as well, as he'll be featured in most of the wedding photos. You may also choose to dress up your ring bearer. Tuxedo measurements are relatively easy to get. Most of the time, anyone can walk into a tailor's shop in his own town and get a free measurement to be e-mailed or phoned into the shop where the tux is rented. Just make sure you have the e-mail or

> Buying a tux will cost from $700 to $2,500. Most are in the $1,200 to $1,500 range.

phone number of that shop so a local tailor can send it in.

When you are looking at tuxedos, there are numerous features to consider. In the end, it's your personal decision that matters most, but first let's sift through some of the parts and styles of a tuxedo:

TUXEDOS

- **Material.** Like any other piece of clothing, you've got a variety of materials to choose from. Most commonly, your choice will be between a synthetic material and wool. Wool definitely carries a more elegant look and feel, though polyesters tend to be cheaper.

- **Style.** Your style will depend first and foremost on the level of formality you desire. Secondly, styles are often paired with what time of day the ceremony will be occurring. Weddings that take place later in the day are traditionally more formal. Depending on these factors, you typically can choose from stroller, cutaway, and tuxedo jackets.

- **Color.** You may want a different color tux than the rest of your groomsmen. However, traditionally, the only variation in the guys' apparel is in accessories. Commonly, the vests or cummerbunds will match the color of the bridesmaid's gown. The color of your boutonniere should complement your bride's bouquet.

- **Accessories.** Here is where you have a little creative freedom. Bowtie, tie, or ascot? Cummerbund or vest?

Now that you know where your choices lie, there are some rules of thumb that you should adhere to when exercising your rights. Most often, your experienced tailor or planner will catch these details, but if not, make sure that you know them when you see them:

SELECTING A TUX

1. **Longevity of the style.** "Look for something that is timeless." says Andonoplas. "Think about looking at the photo years down the road. You don't want to say, 'What was I thinking?'" After looking through your parents' wedding photos, you may have noticed they slipped up on this one. Don't let it happen again.

2. **Feel free to differentiate, but don't let it get out of control.** Try for consistency among the wedding party. You don't want dozens of different colors and styles, or neckties colliding with bow ties. The same goes for shoes. Have all the men wearing matching shoes. Although it's a minute detail, it stands out more than you think. Don't let your wedding look like a prom. Make it look elegant, respectful, organized, and coordinated.

3. **No out-dressing.** Don't let any of your groomsmen outdress their paired bridesmaid, and although it might not be humanly possible, don't out-dress your bride. Let's face it, we men probably don't care about our look as much as the women do, but this is not to say we lack a sense of style. Just make sure that you don't steal the eye of attention from the female participants. You might not hear about it or notice right away, but they will, and you're bound to hear about it soon enough.

Once you and your tailor have decided on a particular style and look for you and your posse, take a deep breath and let your gut hang back out. You've completed your fashion portion of the wedding. But before you leave the shop, make sure you know the answers to these important questions:

- When do the tuxedos have to be returned?
- What is the late return policy?
- What is the policy for missing pieces?
- Do you have someone to drop the tuxes off after the wedding?
- What happens if something doesn't fit when you pick up the tux?

Just in case, when you do go to pick up your tuxedos on your wedding day or the day before, try everything on to be sure your suit fits and that no one's tuxedo bags were switched.

There. These are the areas the groom is typically involved in. It's not all just one giant bachelor party here. Now you can be a well-versed expert and handle it all with skill. Remember your role as an equal participant. There are still plenty of details to be sifted through, and while we all know that you're not the connoisseur of napkin folds that your fiancée is, she'll appreciate any input you can provide. We'll bring you up to speed.

THE OTHER STUFF

H ere we are at the final stages of the wedding, where the groom does not head up the planning committee. But hey, just because you're not the chief doesn't mean you should not have a say. You might think that the man has no place in a flower shop or a bakery picking out cakes. But you might find it surprisingly beneficial to be involved with more than limos, tuxedos, and alcohol. You should pick your cake and eat it too.

As we said previously, planning the wedding is going to get a little stressful. As Dr. Kuhlman noted, simply handing off the wedding responsibilities to your fiancée because you think she would do better at it anyways, or "I don't really have an opinion on that" isn't going to make the situation any better. It's time to form an opinion on flowers and learn a thing or two about the decorations. The less stress the two of you have while planning, the easier it will be to complete the tasks at hand, and the happier you'll be in your relationship. You might even have some extra time to spare, just for the two of you.

Here are some other areas that you may become involved in:

- Reception hall
- Flowers/Decorations
- Bridal gown
- Photography
- Invitations
- Gift registry
- Wedding cake

Although you won't, or may not want, to have a say in some of these details (for example, the bridal gown), we'll teach you what you need to know and what you should ask, plus offer some cost saving tips.

RECEPTION HALL

The reception hall is where it all goes down. This is where you'll cut the cake, Uncle Rudy will pass out in his chair, and your best man will make an honest attempt to cut you down in his toast. For your fiancée, planner, and florist or decorator, there's a lot more that will be involved. They have to envision it from the head table right down to coat check.

There are plenty of places to hold receptions. Reception halls, banquet halls, hotels, country clubs, a local garden or arboretum, a museum, a boat–almost anyplace can be a reception hall now. Many private spaces can be rented out for this occasion as well. Your wedding planner or caterer may have some good ideas for you if you're still looking.

Vital concerns with the reception hall include, of course, your budgetary allotment, but also the seating capacity. You've got 400 people invited to your wedding? It might be difficult to find a boat, then. Once you've found some place that matches your budget and size needs, think about logistics. How far from the ceremony is it? Are the guests going to run into traffic, so the trip will take an hour? Find someplace close so guests can instantly unwind after the ceremony and prepare to celebrate more intimately with you.

Besides getting your guests to the reception, think about transporting the rest of the materials for your reception. If you are looking at a hotel or other all-inclusive location, they most likely have their own catering staff, which may mean they expect to provide everything you need, from coconut shrimp to chair covers. This can be an advantage or disadvantage, depending on whether you want to use what they have to offer.

QUESTIONS TO ASK ABOUT THE RECEPTION HALL

- Can you bring food in or does it need to be catered by that facility? You can't eat Burger King at a McDonald's.
- Can you bring your own cake in? (Sometimes they may have their own bakery department.)
- What's included in the set-up? Tables and chairs? A gift table? A cake table?

- What extra fees apply? Is there a parking fee for the guests? What are the taxes?
- If you are bringing food in, what time can the vendor begin bringing it in? What time can they set up?

Choosing the venue is a large decision and often, once it's decided, a lot of other decisions fall together soon after. If you've chosen an all-inclusive venue that won't let you bring in food or beverages from any other service, then most likely your decisions for catering, a wedding cake, and alcohol have just been made, too. This is why choosing a location is important. Remember, it's one of Frank's Big Four identified in the previous chapter–when, where, how much to spend, and how many people? This is your "where." Try and have this arranged, depending on the popularity of your location and date, one year in advance. Don't be surprised if you choose a popular location and they're booked solid for the next two years, however. If you have a shorter engagement, don't worry. With enough research and visits to reception halls, you should discover great available venues. The only time where we have seen problems with short notice is in small towns, where there may only be one or two locations that can hold a wedding, but larger cities always have some great reception sites waiting to be discovered.

FLOWERS/DECORATIONS

While flowers tend to symbolize and embody beauty, grace, and romance, there's plenty of room for masculinity here, too. If you skip out on the flower consultation and don't throw in your ideas, you may end up standing in the middle of a pink and purple wedding that is a little too feminine for your tastes. Make some suggestions and add your own flavor. Bridal consultant Frank Andonoplas reports that when talking to his brides and grooms, the most common request from the brides is for pink flowers. He often suggests pairing the pink with a more masculine color, such as brown.

When dragged into the flower shop, what do you need to know? How does this whole flower consultation work? Well, first you need to decide a few things with your partner.

DECORATION CONSIDERATIONS

1. **Color Scheme.** What colors will your wedding be based on?
2. **Style.** Is your wedding modern, contemporary and cutting-edge, or traditional and romantic? Is there a theme?
3. **Budget.** How much are you willing to spend? Flowers will cost anywhere up to $30,000, with the average at around $2,500 to $3,000.

Now that those decisions have been made, you're ready to pick a florist. Depending on whether or not your wedding is on a busy day or season, you should try to get the flower decisions made about six to nine months prior to your ceremony date. If it's a really busy day and/or location, say Valentine's Day in New York, then you'll want to book your florist at least a year in advance. To shop around, you should not only base your pick on costs, but also on a couple of other considerations:

- How long have they been designing? It takes a skilled eye to coordinate and arrange and a veteran to know the time frame for moving and setting up, so experience is key!

6 to 9 Months Ahead

Choose a florist

- How many weddings do they do per weekend and/or week? You may want a more personalized service through someone who has fewer weddings on their schedule. However, a florist that books lots of gigs is probably popular for a reason.

- What does the price include? Will your florist move the flowers from the ceremony to the reception?

- What is the florist's unique selling point? What sets them apart from others? See what your florist's creative edge is. It might be the perfect touch to make your ceremony and reception special.

- Do they provide a contract? Many florists will not, and instead just jot down your orders on a pad. Protect yourself from disaster and go with a florist with a contract, or at least insist on having a copy of your decisions in writing.

- What's in-season, and how could you use that to get the best value? Ordering out-of-season flowers can be expensive.

Now that you've picked out a florist, convey your color scheme, style or theme, and your budgeted allowance. Allow them to see linens you chose with your caterer (right down to the napkins!) to avoid any clashing colors. Once you have made your ideas clear, listen to what recommendations your florist has. Ask to see photos of what they suggest. Don't suffocate their creativity though. "Let them come up with ideas . . . The florist needs some creative, artistic license, if you will," says California florist Marcia L. Johnson.

Don't get stuck thinking that flowers are just bunched together and placed on the middle of tables. There are lots of interesting things your florist can do. Some of Johnson's creative touches involve hanging flowers and crystals from trees or making sphere balls out of flowers. She has even made purses out of flowers for the bridesmaids and flower girls. See if the florist can match your decorations and your wedding's style and personality.

After you've come up with something, ask for the estimated price. "A good florist should let you walk away with the line item pricing," says Johnson. Some may have to get back to you in a couple days or a week. If the price is a bit too high for you, opt to cut your costs by using more in-season flowers and/or keeping the centerpieces and décor simpler.

BRIDAL GOWN

In the bridal gown department, there's not much room for the groom's advice. There's so much more that goes into a woman's apparel than a man's. We're sure that if you've ever wanted to dress up to go somewhere in a hurry, you've already learned this lesson. It's going to be a highly specialized subject far beyond your fashion sense, and often your advice pertaining to how that dress should fit is not appreciated. The bridal gown is one area of the wedding where, traditionally, you have no say.

Not allowing the groom to see the dress before the wedding is a long-established tradition. This applies to the picking out of the dress, the alterations, the rehearsal and rehearsal dinner, continuing all the way until you hear them start to play *Here Comes the Bride*. She hides the beauty until your day and presents it as a gift. When you turn to see her at the doors, she wants you to be stunned, absolutely stunned.

Besides, if she is like many women, she already has her wedding gown designed in her head, and your suggestions are superfluous at best, disastrous at worst. The gown may or may not be in your budget. Often, the bride's parents pay for it. If the gown is something the two of you are paying for, then you might be stuck reminding her of the budget while trying to accommodate her dreams.

There are a few ways that you can save money in this area. Remember, don't attack her dreams, but if she's open to it (and you'd know above all), then mentioning these ideas could be worth a try.

Does her mother still have her wedding dress? If so, what does your fiancée think of it? Sure, style changes every year and that dress may be out of date. However, your fiancée may love it! If she does, then there's a strong possibility that, with a couple of alterations, you've got a free bridal gown.

Are there any discount bridal shops in town? When most bridal gown shops say they have used bridal dresses, they don't mean the gowns sold back from divorces. Often, the term "used" means the dresses were display models, meaning they've been in a window display or shown off by a model. If she's really set on shopping for a new one, though, don't push the used option. You'll surely regret telling her that you are more concerned about money than making her dreams

> If she is like many women, she already has her wedding gown designed in her head, and your suggestions are superfluous at best, disastrous at worst.

come true. Instead, kindly remind her (maybe prior to the moment she is stepping out the door) what the budget for the gown is and tell her that she is looking absolutely gorgeous. When she leaves with her friends, then you can silently pray.

PHOTOGRAPHER/VIDEOGRAPHER

How do you want your wedding moments to be remembered? In photos? In a video? Or both? This is something you should plan early on. Photographers and videographers have only so many weekends and they book up fast. Don't wait until the last minute on this one.

There are a couple of things you need to consider when meeting with prospective photographers.

1. What style are you looking for? Many photographers offer or specialize in either posed photos or photojournalism. Photojournalists try to capture stories through more candid shots. Make sure your photographer can handle whichever you prefer.
2. What equipment will the photographer be using? Digital, 35mm film, or other? Many photographers will stick to their guns and insist that what they use is top of the line, but if you have a preference, that should be a priority.
3. How long will the pre-wedding photo shoot take? This is important for scheduling, because you'll have plenty to do that day. Make sure to contact your photographer again a week ahead of your wedding to go over the schedule once more.

An alternative or addition to photography, videography is a great way to capture more of the wedding. Here, too, there are different styles and approaches you can choose. You can add special effects and a soundtrack or have it more documentary-style, unscripted, as the story unfolds. You may consider having the videographer include some of your wedding

QUESTIONS TO ASK THE PHOTOGRAPHER

1. Will you be the photographer actually covering the event?
2. What will you be wearing? If your photographer is going to be running around the ceremony while you exchange vows, you don't want him wearing a bright orange sweater. Some will attempt to match the wedding party.
3. Will guests be able to take flash photography?
4. How long will you be at the event?
5. What does the price include and what extras does it include (e.g. additional prints of the photos, an album, etc.)?
6. When will the photos be ready?

photos in the video. Here you will, as with the photographer, book early and ask almost the same questions. It may be worth exploring the option of having the engagement proceedings taped by the videographer as well, to get a more encompassing video, including maybe dress fittings, rehearsal dinners, all the way up to the ceremony.

Photography and videography will each cost $3,000 to $5,000, or more.

INVITATIONS

When your wedding date is still far off in the future, it's important to get invitations out early enough to allow your guests the chance to adjust their schedules accordingly. Do not underestimate the undertaking invitations involve. Any do-it-yourself-er is going to want to save a buck on this

4 Months Ahead

Send save-the-dates

detail and suggest that invitations be homemade. You may have a computer with graphics software and a printer, along with some nice textured paper, but believe us: In most situations, you won't have the time to pull it off. "It's going to be hours and hours," said Megan Kuntze of Crane Stationery, a leader in the invitations vendor industry. Their blue book on writing etiquette remains a standard for how to present the couple through the invitations. "Why not leave it to the professionals, who have the time, so that you can still contribute and have your ideas put in, [while] taking out the hardest part and giving that piece to someone who knows how to execute it?" adds Kuntze.

Before you even begin thinking about the invitations, Kuntze suggests that you start thinking about a "save-the-date" notice. This is a small reminder sent out to your guests at least four months prior (a year is preferred) so that they may clear their schedules. You may not need this for a smaller wedding, but your guests will appreciate the advance notice.

The world of invitations has been transformed over the past couple years. Traditionally, invitations were the responsibility of the bride's family. Now that more couples are paying for their own weddings or sharing the cost with their families, everyone can have a say in the invitations. The design has evolved from simple black text on white or ecru stationery, to engraved typeface in any color onto textured or even cloth mediums. There's a lot to choose from, so get in there and throw in your ideas along with your fiancée's.

You should be consulting a stationery vendor six months to a year in advance. Find someone you are comfortable working with and arrange a meeting. Because of the invitation design explosion over the past years, looking through albums of previous work can be overwhelming; there is so much to choose from. "[T]hat consultant is going to try and determine what your tastes are, and then they're going to guide you to an album that goes along with your taste level," says Kuntze. Be sure to convey as many stylistic details of the wedding as best you can, such as color schemes, location, and any themes. These aspects of the wedding will dictate what your invitation should look like.

6 Months to a Year Ahead

Consult a stationery vendor

Once you've located a design in the album, the consultant should guide you through the rest of the process. You can now choose the type-face, the printing technique—engraved, ther-mography (raised lettering), flat printing, colors, et cetera. There are plenty of creative twists you include with your invitations. A recent trend in invitation is to create "minifolders." Treat your out-of-town guests to a guide of happenings and directions for their weekend stay. Include direc-tions to local sites of interest or entertainment, directions to the wedding and ceremony, and or a schedule of events, such as dinners for guests that you'll be attending. If you are doing some-thing like a honeymoon registry (talked about in next section) you will want to send that along with your invitations. For more of a personal touch, Kuntze has been a long-time advocate of addressing the invitations yourself, as opposed to having the stationer print them out on envelopes. "It really adds a beautiful and personal touch to have those addresses handwritten."

After you've made your decisions, you should ask your stationer a few questions:

1. How long will it take to get my invitations?
2. Can you show me exactly how they're supposed to be packaged in the envelope?
3. What else should I be thinking of buying at this time? Thank you notes? Couples' stationery? "We're moving" cards?

Your invitations will probably cost you anywhere from $300 to $5,000. If you just can't get over the idea of saving money on invitations, there are a couple of routes you can take to cut corners. Re-think printing techniques; engraving and letter press can be quite expensive. "You can save your costs if you go to thermography, and the same with flat printing," says Kuntze. You can also save by having fewer pieces in your invitation. The reception card should be the first to go. This card gives directions to the reception and is separate from the card with the directions to the ceremony. "I think that's evolved because typically everyone that's been invited has been invited to both events." She added a warning, though: "Don't try and cut your costs by not choosing the most beautiful paper." Crane uses 100 percent cotton paper, for example. "People know it the minute they pull it out of their mailbox," she explains. "*That's* the kind of impression you want to make."

No matter what, don't e-mail invitations. You wouldn't want to have guests miss out because of their spam filter or an accidental keystroke. What would guests without access to Internet do? Your wedding should be a lasting, unforgettable event. A quick e-mail is not representative of the intimacy of the affair.

GIFT REGISTRY

Probably the easiest part of the engagement process is the gift registry, which is like a Christmas wish list for your wedding. Many large chain stores, such as Target, J.C. Penney's, and even Home Depot have registries available. These registries will save guests from guessing on what gifts to get you and will help you keep a coordinated style for household products, among other things. Before you create a registry, though, make sure to take an inventory of what items you and your fiancée already have. After you've made an inventory, you're ready to start your registry list.

It is best to choose at least one or two large chain stores in your area. This helps your out-of-town guests, who most likely have a Sears nearby, but maybe not a Ted's Appliances. Begin by telling customer service you'd like to create a registry. They may have you use an in-store computer system or a scanner to select items as you come across them. Many of these stores also have listings online that you can create while sitting at home.

Some people are confused as to what to put on the list, but really, there are no rules. Include some essentials, things you'll need when you start out in your new home or start to live together as husband and wife. However, don't feel like you can't throw in some nonessential gifts. Some guests may want to buy you something you can really have fun with, such as a television or kayak, or books. Many travel agencies also create honeymoon registries; you can send a card with your

> **Tip**
> It is best to choose at least one or two large chain stores in your area. This helps your out-of-town guests, who most likely have a Sears nearby, but maybe not a Ted's Appliances.

6 Months Ahead

Schedule a cake tasting

invitation, and guests can simply donate to your "honeymoon fund" instead of buying a gift. While the sky is the limit, make sure to be realistic. Don't put expensive gifts on the list that none or few of your guests will be able to afford. If you and your fiancée come from different socioeconomic backgrounds, creating a list that accommodates only one side can create some very unnecessary tension. If this is the case, create a registry that is broad and encompasses the entire spectrum, perhaps a combination of a few expensive gifts and many smaller gifts. Either way, be grateful, and appreciate every gift you receive.

WEDDING CAKE

The wedding cake is a great centerpiece to your wedding. It's not just about the delicious and moist center or the frosting, but the tradition that's baked in. The cutting of the cake is a sign that the formalities are over. Sharing that first piece represents the promise of a whole new life together. The cake is an important piece of the reception and not just a delicious dessert. As with the invitations, the wedding cake can seem a likely candidate for saving money. Be warned— after a couple of accidents, having a friend make it or doing it yourself can cost you more money than just having a pro create it in the first place. Better safe than sorry; go with a pro.

Be sure to call local bakeries at least six months before the wedding. Keep in mind that the end of the week, Thursday through Saturday, tends to be the busiest for bakeries, so call early in the week to see if your wedding date is open. If the date is open, schedule a meeting with someone on staff to view the cakes and taste some of their flavors. Next, you'll be able to look through a portfolio of past work and see whether or not your ideas match their abilities.

QUESTIONS TO ASK YOUR BAKER

■ **Delivery.** Is this included in the cost? You're not going to have the time to take care of this. There is plenty of expertise involved in transporting this delicate creation, as you can probably imagine. Either way, professional delivery is worth the extra $40 over a damaged 200-person, $8 per slice cake on your wedding day.

■ **Accident recovery.** If there is an accident with your delivery, will delivery personnel be able to make emergency decoration repair?

■ **Price.** How much per slice for my design? Will we have to rent toppers, stands, etc. for the cake?

Wedding cakes can be expensive; they are very labor- and time-intensive. Typically, you'll be paying from $1,000 to $5,000 on average, for a 200-person cake. There are many ways you can cut costs to get a great cake on the lower price of the spectrum. If you are interested in saving money, ask your baker if any of the following tips can be implemented in the cake design.

■ **Real flowers.** They cost much less than sugar flowers and weigh less, needing less of a foundation. Many times a florist can use the leftovers from your decorations. Just make sure they have no toxins on them that could bleed into the frosting.

- **Smaller show cake.** Instead of having one large, tiered cake, use several. Have one smaller cake for show and then numerous sheet cakes in the back room to feed the rest of the guests. There will be less design-time involved. Better yet, you can make several small cakes and use them as the centerpieces at each table.
- **Styrofoam tiers.** If you want a multi-tier cake for show, then you may be able to substitute iced Styrofoam layers at a fraction of the cost.
- **Unconventional approaches.** Cupcakes, pies, and cheesecakes arranged in tiers can substitute for the more traditional cake.

The planning of a wedding is a time consuming and vigorous operation. Most likely, you'll feel like you've taken on a second job. There will be plenty of stress over these details, and it's easy to get overwhelmed. However, it's a chance for you to prove to your fiancée just what she can expect out of you as a husband. With the added stress, it's easy to push these details onto your fiancée and convince yourself that she is more interested in them than you. Show her that she's marrying a man who has an undying dedication to and diligence for the relationship. Show her she isn't agreeing to be with just a huge football fan or handyman for the rest of her life–she's marrying a companion, a teammate, a soul mate. Besides, it's your wedding, too.

COUNT DOWN TO THE WEDDING CHECKLIST

12 MONTHS BEFORE

- ❏ Announce your engagement to family and close friends
- ❏ Send your announcement to local newspapers
- ❏ Dedicate a planning notebook or other organization tool
- ❏ Develop a guest list

11 MONTHS BEFORE

- ❏ Plan a preliminary budget (use the one in the back of this book to help)
- ❏ Research wedding and reception locations
- ❏ Select bridal and groom parties and ask each person to participate

10 MONTHS BEFORE

- ❏ Set your date
- ❏ Book the wedding and reception location ASAP
- ❏ Interview and select caterer, photographer, florist, music, videographer

9 MONTHS BEFORE

- ❏ Mail, "save the date" cards to guests
- ❏ Register for gifts
- ❏ Bride should be looking at dresses

8 MONTHS BEFORE

- ❏ Interview and select who will preside over the ceremony
- ❏ Interview cake designers, sample cakes, and select your cake
- ❏ Begin to review honeymoon locations
- ❏ Finalize budget

7 MONTHS BEFORE

- ❏ Bride should order her wedding dress
- ❏ Bride begins to select bridesmaid dresses
- ❏ Finalize guest list

6 MONTHS BEFORE

- ❏ Begin shopping for invitations and stationery
- ❏ Place order for bridesmaid dresses and accessories
- ❏ Bride and groom's mother select dresses
- ❏ Reserve rental equipment (chairs, arches, linens, etc.)
- ❏ Order invitations and stationery
- ❏ Research and book your rehearsal dinner location

5 MONTHS BEFORE

- ❏ Select wedding favors
- ❏ Shop for wedding rings
- ❏ Finalize your décor ideas and shop for decorations
- ❏ Begin shopping for groom's wedding attire
- ❏ Send tux measurement forms to groomsmen
- ❏ Start picking dates for the bachelor party

4 MONTHS BEFORE

- ❏ Finalize flowers
- ❏ Order tuxes
- ❏ Book honeymoon
- ❏ Purchase groom's gift
- ❏ Book block of rooms for out-of-town guests

3 MONTHS BEFORE

- ❏ Plan seating arrangements for reception
- ❏ Purchase wedding accessories: guest book, ring bearer pillow, toasting glasses, unity candle, flower basket, serving set
- ❏ Solidify time and date for the bachelor party

2 MONTHS BEFORE
- ❏ Mail invitations
- ❏ Apply for marriage license
- ❏ Choose or write vows

1 MONTH BEFORE
- ❏ Finalize ceremony plans
- ❏ Submit wedding program to stationer
- ❏ Finalize transportation of family, party and out-of-town guests
- ❏ Pick up wedding rings
- ❏ Get forms for name change on driver's license, Social Security card, passport, insurance and medical plans, and bank accounts

3 WEEKS BEFORE
- ❏ Reconfirm hotel reservations for guests as well as for honeymoon
- ❏ Purchase and print dinner seating cards for guests

2 WEEKS BEFORE
- ❏ Pack for honeymoon
- ❏ Send final payment to suppliers
- ❏ Get your hair cut

1 WEEK BEFORE
- ❏ Pick up your tux
- ❏ Make time to relax
- ❏ Attend rehearsal and rehearsal dinner

COST WORKSHEET

	PERCENTAGE	YOUR COST
ATTIRE Bride Accessories Groom Accessories Groom Tux/Suit Hair & Makeup Headpiece/Veil Wedding Dress	7%	
CEREMONY Ceremony Accessories Ceremony Location Ceremony Site Decorations Marriage License Officiate Rehearsal Dinner	9%	
FAVORS & GIFTS Attendant Gifts Parent Gifts Wedding Favors	4%	
FLOWERS Boutonnieres/Corsages Bride Bouquet Bridesmaid Bouquets Flower Girl Flowers Flowers (Ceremony & Reception)	4%	
JEWELRY His & Her Rings	6%	

	PERCENTAGE	YOUR COST
MUSIC Reception Band/Disc Jockey	3%	
PHOTOGRAPHY & VIDEO Photographer Videographer	10%	
RECEPTION Bride/Groom Hotel Reception Beverages/Bartender Reception Decorations/Centerpieces Reception Food Service Reception Venue/Rentals Wedding Cake	51%	
STATIONERY Invitations & Reply Cards Other Stationery	3%	
TRANSPORTATION Limo/Car Rental	3%	
TOTAL COST	100%	